973.5 M /BHPJ/211466
Meltzer, Milton,
Hunted like a wolf; the story of the Sem
3 5048 00028 4917

Y0-BDJ-080

DATE			

HUNTED LIKE A WOLF

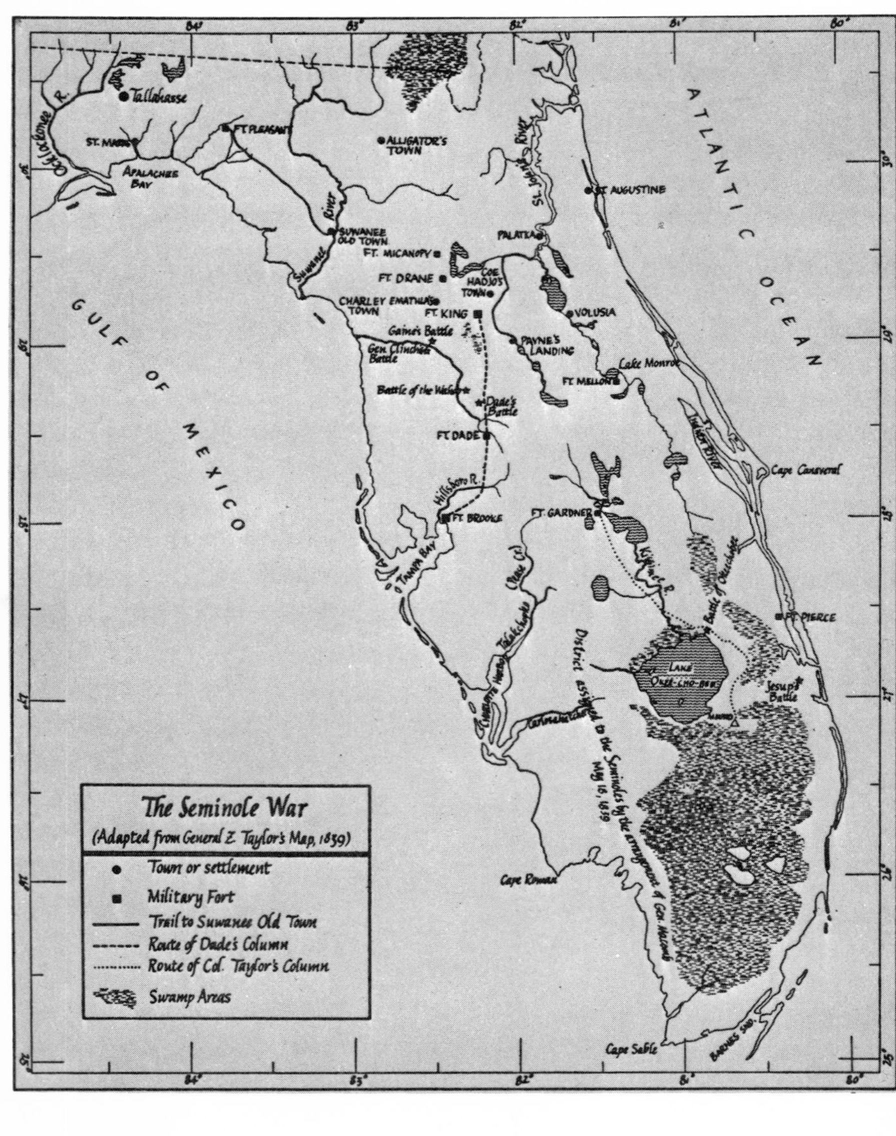

The Seminole War
(Adapted from General Z. Taylor's Map, 1839)
Town or settlement
Military Fort
Trail to Suwanee Old Town
Route of Dade's Column
Route of Col. Taylor's Column
Swamp Areas
84°
83°
82°
81°
80°
30°
29°
28°
27°
26°
25°
Ocklockonee R.
Tallahasse
ST. MARKS
FT. PLEASANT
APALACHEE BAY
ALLIGATOR'S TOWN
St. John's River
ST. AUGUSTINE
ATLANTIC OCEAN
Suwanee River
SUWANEE OLD TOWN
PALATKA
FT. MICANOPY
FT. DRANE
COE HADJO'S TOWN
CHARLEY EMATHLA'S TOWN
FT. KING
VOLUSIA
GULF OF MEXICO
Gaine's Battle
Gen. Clinch's Battle
PAYNE'S LANDING
Lake Monroe
FT. MELLON
Battle of the Withlacoochee
Dade's Battle
FT. DADE
Indian River
Cape Canaveral
Hillsboro R.
FT. BROOKE
FT. GARDNER
TAMPA BAY
Peace Cr.
Kissimee R.
Battle of Okeechobee
FT. PIERCE
Talakchopko
District assigned to the Seminoles by the arrangement of Gen. Macomb May 18, 1839
LAKE OKEE-CHO-BEE
Jesup's Battle
Charlotte Harbor
Caloosahatchee
Cape Romano
Cape Sable
BARNES SND.

HUNTED LIKE A WOLF

The Story of the Seminole War

Milton Meltzer

Farrar, Straus and Giroux/New York
[c1972]

First printing, 1972
Library of Congress catalog card number: 72-78464
ISBN: 0-374-33521-4
Published simultaneously in Canada by
Doubleday Canada Ltd., Toronto
Printed in the United States of America
Designed by Sheila Lynch

"I have been hunted like a wolf and now I am about to be sent away like a dog."

—Halleck, a Seminole leader
July 1842

Contents

HUNTED LIKE A WOLF

1

Three Choices

It began with Christopher Columbus.

He was looking for riches—gold, silver, spices, sugar, silks, perfumes, drugs—and for converts to Christianity, when he "discovered" America. It was a New World. New to Columbus, but not to its millions of dark-skinned peoples. They had been there for thousands of years before the white man "discovered" them. Columbus called them "Indians" because he mistakenly thought he had landed on the islands of the Indies, off the coast of Asia.

He was amazed at the sight of the Indians. "They all go naked as their mothers bore them," he wrote, "and the women also. . . . Some of them paint their faces, some of them their whole bodies, some only the nose." He was pleased to find they had no means of defending themselves: "They do not bear arms or know them for I showed them swords and they took them by the blades and cut themselves through ignorance. . . . These people are very unskilled in arms. . . . With fifty men they could all be subjected and made to do all that I wished."

Their generous ways puzzled him: "Anything they have, if it be asked for they never say no, but rather invite the person to accept it, and show as much lovingness as though they would give their hearts."

But as soon as he finished exclaiming over how kind, peaceful, and generous the Indians were, Columbus wrote back to Spain, to King Ferdinand and Queen Isabella, who had sponsored his voyage: "From here, in the name of the Blessed Trinity, we can send all the slaves that can be sold. [The Indians] are fit to be ordered about and made to work."

He put five hundred Tainos on caravels and sent them to Spain. Almost half died on the long voyage. The survivors were sold in the slave market of Seville, but they, too, soon died. It would be more profitable, he thought, to use Indian slave labor in the Americas. They were put to extracting gold from the river beds. But many fled to the mountains. Those who stayed died quickly in slavery, or revolted. Columbus punished them with torture or executions. His men took hounds and hunted the fugitives down in the mountains. Thousands of Indians poisoned themselves rather than give in.

Death was wholesale. In 1492 the Indian population of the island of Hispaniola was estimated to be 300,000. Fifty years later a Spaniard reported only five hundred Indians were left.

The Spaniards were only the first. Soon the Portuguese and many other Europeans sailed across the seas to plunder the Americas. "People from heaven," the Indians at first called them, welcoming them, often helping them to set up their colonies. They soon learned how cruel and greedy the strangers were.

A pattern of plantations gradually grew up in the New World. The pattern grew out of experience the Europeans had had in colonies of the Mediterranean and the Atlantic. To make profits on the sugar, cotton, and tobacco plantations, production had to be on a large scale. And for that, plenty of cheap labor was needed.

Slaves were the answer for the white settlers. They began with the people they found in the Caribbean islands—the Indians—and, when the Indians had almost been wiped out, imported Africans.

Columbus knew nothing about the people he found living in the New World. He did not realize they were not a single people but many different peoples. There were about thirty million Indians then in South America, and about one million in North America. They lived in hundreds of different societies. In physical appearance, in culture, in language, they varied as widely as the people who lived in the Old World.

But Columbus and most of the white explorers and colonizers who came after him were not able to see that. They saw the natives through a European looking glass; the image was badly distorted. The whites debated whether the Indians were humankind. Some said

Indians were a sort of two-legged animal without soul or spirit. If the Indian was subhuman, then the white man need have no qualms about killing him.

Unable to understand the Indians, the Europeans called them savages or barbarians. (Every people has found it hard to appreciate the customs, culture, and religion of another people. It was true of the Egyptians, the Greeks, the Romans, the Chinese. It is still true.)

What the Indians were like in that part of the New World which became the United States is much better understood today. Most of us picture the Indian with high cheekbones, an eagle-beak nose, and reddish-brown skin. But the Indians were not a uniform group when the Europeans came. Some scientists believe that the native Americans were the result of the ancient intermingling of ethnic groups. Or at first they may have been a relatively uniform people, who developed into separate groups through isolation, genetic change, and intermixture.

The Indians were divided not only by language and culture but by physical appearance. One group might be heavy-bearded and round-faced, while another might be lightly bearded and sharp-featured. From one region to another of the vast continent, many variations in color, eye, nose, height, build could be found. Great differences sometimes occurred even among Indian groups who lived not far from one another.

Some Indians lived in well-built houses of logs, planks, or adobe; some in many-roomed long houses of bark; some in earth lodges; some in multistoried communal pueblos. Many lived in towns or villages. Only some, such as the nomadic hunters of the plains, used the hide-covered tepee that almost every moviegoer thinks of as the typical Indian dwelling.

The Indians provided for their family and their tribe by hunting, fishing, or farming. The men usually did the hunting and fishing, and made the tools and weapons. The women raised the crops, cooked, made the clothes, took care of the children. They sought to have enough to live on, not to get rich.

The Indians knew how to grow plants and they steadily improved upon them by seed selection, by soil culture, and by the use of fertilizers. The white man learned to grow corn properly from the Indian. Indian farmers raised sweet potatoes, tomatoes, pumpkins, peanuts, squash, chili peppers, beans, and many other crops. It was Indians who introduced tobacco to the whites. Indians developed cotton independently from efforts to raise it in the Old World. They devised complex irrigation systems that made farming possible in desert regions.

Metals such as copper, bronze, iron, and steel were unknown to the Indians. The tools they used for farming, fishing, hunting, and war were made of stone, bone, or wood. Indian clothing was usually made of hides or furs, with moccasins the chief footgear.

The forms of Indian life were as richly varied as the language and cultural patterns. The rigid social structures of the Aztecs and Mayas were unknown north of Central America. Most of the North American Indians would not submit themselves to such ironbound control.

War among the Indians was nothing like that conducted by armies ruled by military leaders. War raids were usually made on the initiative of an individual. Some tribes warred against each other, and some joined forces as allies. But there were Indian groups who did not approve of war and would fight only when attacked.

The Indians held the land in common. No Indian had the exclusive right to own or use a piece of land, to give it away or to sell it. That was a concept the white man brought which the Indian did not understand. To the Indians the land was for all. They had a reverence for the earth and its web of life. They saw man as linked to the universe, partner in its vitality.

But to the white colonist this view was alien. The white American was ambitious and aggressive. He would let nothing stand in the way of his goal: to acquire land and wealth. Isaac Weld, the English traveler, visiting the United States soon after its birth, wrote that the government and its people

> looked upon them [the Indians] . . . merely as wild beasts, that ought to be banished from the face of the earth; and actuated by the insatiable spirit of avarice, and that restless and dissatisfied turn of mind, which I have so frequently noticed; instead of keeping within their territories, where millions of acres remained unoccupied, but no part,

however, of which could be had without being paid for, they crossed their boundary lines, and fixed themselves in the territory of the Indians, without ever previously gaining the consent of these people.

From the beginning, English colonists believed Indians were hardly human and therefore the land they lived upon was open territory to be grabbed at will. William Bradford in 1617, looking across the sea to the land where the Puritans would found their Plymouth Colony, saw "the vast and unpeopled countries of America which are fruitful and fit for habitation, being devoid of all civil inhabitants, where there are only savages and brutish men, which range up and down, little otherwise than the wild beasts of the same."

Two hundred and fifty years later, it was no different. At an Indian council in 1877, Sitting Bull said:

Hear me, people, we have now to deal with another race—small and feeble when our fathers first met them but now great and overbearing. Strangely enough, they have a mind to till the soil and the love of possession is a disease with them. . . . They claim this mother of ours, the earth, for their own and fence their neighbors away; they deface her with their buildings and their refuse. That nation is like a spring freshet that overruns its banks and destroys all who are in its path.

We cannot dwell side by side. Only seven years ago we made a treaty by which we were assured that the buffalo country should be left to us forever. Now they threaten to take that away from us. My brothers, shall we submit or shall we say to them: "First kill me before you take possession of my Fatherland."

The Indian had no rights the white man was bound to respect—except the right to be converted to Christianity. As early as 1583, one English backer of colonization, Sir George Peckham, knew what was good for the Indians: "The savages are to be brought from falsehood to truth, from darkness to light, from the highway of death to the path of life, from superstitious idolatry to sincere Christianity, from the devil to Christ, from hell to heaven."

The white man, believing himself superior to the Indian, felt he had a mission: to make the Indian over in the white man's image, to convert the Indian from his own faith to the white man's religion, to get him to drop his own customs and to adopt the white man's ways. "The nasty savages," as Charles Chauncy, president of Harvard University, saw them in 1664, needed to be taught how to live and what to think.

Among the baggage the white man carried with him to these shores was the belief that his skin color made him superior. In his mind colored people were inferior to white. He identified the red man and the black man with evil, with savagery. It gave him an excuse for enslaving or killing Indians and blacks. Colored people were good only for doing the hard and dirty work the white man did not want to do.

Racist beliefs became woven into custom and law, into religion and education. Each white generation learned from preacher and teacher that colored people were inferior. Slavery and segregation were, therefore, natural and necessary. The first was a means of getting useful labor from people fit for nothing else. And the second was a way to keep them from contaminating their betters.

How did the Indians feel about the whites who came to live on their continent? In 1787 a Delaware chief named Pachgantachilias said:

> I admit there are good white men, but they bear no proportion to the bad; the bad must be the strongest for they rule. They do what they please. They enslave those who are not of their color, although created by the same Great Spirit who created them. They would make slaves of us if they could; but as they cannot do it, they kill us. There is no faith to be placed in their words.
>
> They are not like the Indians who are only enemies while at war, and are friends in peace. They will say to an Indian, "My friend, my brother!" They will take him by the hand and, at the same moment, destroy him. And you will also be treated by them before long. Remember that this day I warned you to beware of such friends as these. I know the Long-knives. They are not to be trusted.

Whatever the culture the Indians had—"savage" or "civilized"—it did not really matter to the white invaders. The whites, as Sitting Bull said, claimed the American earth for their own and would destroy anyone who stood in their way.

What were the Indians to do? Give up the land they lived on? Resist the whites? Or try to stay where they were, but living apart, in states of their own?

As soon as the whites had stayed in any place long enough to show their intentions, the Indians began to debate what they should do. It always came to deciding on one of these three courses of action. If they took the first path, it meant abandoning their tribal lands and their ancient ways of living. They would have "to walk in the ways of the white man."

To resist meant war. And war—against an enemy so superior in numbers and in weapons—would mean extermination.

The third choice meant confining themselves to limited areas, in communities apart from the white man, while he did what he liked on the rest of the land. But for that to work, the white had to be willing to live and let live. He had to respect agreements concerning territorial limits and the rights of independent Indian states.

Bitter arguments took place among the Indians. It was hard to find unanimous agreement on what policy to follow. (This discord was another gift of the whites to the Indians.) From colonial times on, the whites took advantage of such differences. They made pawns of Indian tribes. The English, the French, the Spanish, the Americans, used one group of Indians to fight against another. Brother shed brother's blood in the interest of the whites. Such was the case in the French and Indian Wars, the American Revolution, and the War of 1812. The whites came to dominate the New World by getting one group of Indians to conquer another.

Under relentless pressure from the whites, the Indians signed treaties. Almost always, at the heart of each treaty was the giving up of some Indian land, in return for money or other land. Rarely were Indians paid the true value of their land. Deceit and treachery often played a part in the whites' negotiation of treaties. If the Indians refused to sign, they were made to do so by force they could not withstand.

When Indians would not move off their lands, the whites made war. From the settlement of Jamestown to the end of the nineteenth century, some two hundred major battles were fought between Indians and whites. Again and again the Indians chose to die fighting rather than submit to the white man. Twice in Virginia—in 1622 and 1644—Opecanacanough led uprisings. In New England, the Pequot War took place in 1637 and King Philip's War in 1672–76. In the Southeast, the Creek War of 1813–14 was another major conflict.

Battles and skirmishes by the hundreds cost blood and life until 1890. The Indian Wars, they were called, but it was really all one great war, lasting some three hundred years, punctuated by almost four hundred treaties, few or none of them kept.

One chapter in this tragic story—one of the least written about but one of the most significant—was the

Seminole War of 1835–42. It was the longest of the Indian Wars, and the costliest in money and human life. At issue this time were not only Indian lands and Indian rights but, equally, the fate of black people—many of them runaway slaves—whom the Seminole had taken in and befriended. In the story of the Seminole War can be seen all the forces of America's terrible racial history.

2

A New Indian Nation

Florida, that big paw of the American continent dipping into the warm waters of the Atlantic and the Gulf of Mexico, became the battleground of the Seminole War. Less than twenty-five years after Columbus's first voyage to America, Spanish voyagers visited the coast of Florida, giving Florida the distinction of being America's oldest frontier. The Spanish occupied the peninsula for almost three centuries.

The Seminole Indians were not there when the Spanish arrived. It was the Calusa Indians of southern Florida who saw the three caravels of Ponce de León when they sailed in looking for slaves and gold. Stories of kidnappings and killings by strange white men in the Bahamas and the southern islands had already reached the Calusa; the big seagoing trading canoes carried the news fast. The Florida Indians knew what the Spanish in these first slaving ships wanted, and from the earliest recorded times they resisted the white man's attempts to send them to the West Indies to replace the native slave labor which was rapidly being killed off. Spaniards unlucky enough to be shipwrecked off coasts the Calusa controlled were killed or in turn enslaved by them.

It was an unequal contest. The Calusa numbered perhaps fifteen thousand when the Spanish came. After 1572, little was heard of the Calusa again. The Apalachees, too, disappeared before white invasion, this time by the English. Many were captured and sold into slavery in the West Indies. The Timucuans, who lived in northeastern and central Florida when the Spanish arrived, were wiped out by the invaders' guns and diseases or by Carolina slave raiders.

By the early 1800's, wars and slave raids had eliminated Florida's aborigines as tribes. Scattered remnants survived, to become fused with the Seminole.

Who were the Seminole? Relatively young among Indian nations, they consisted primarily of groups who broke away from the Creeks in Georgia. They began migrating to north Florida in the early 1700's and came in three successive waves over the next hundred years.

Seminole life developed out of Creek ways, which were very different from those of the Florida aborigines. Creek culture was first described by Hernando de Soto. His was the most famous of the early Spanish expeditions to Florida. His ten ships beached at Tampa Bay in 1539. With about six hundred soldiers and a few women, his army headed north on mules and horses, driving before them their live food supply—poultry, pigs, sheep, and cattle. They explored a region now included in several Southeastern states.

In what was to be Alabama and Mississippi, de Soto found Indians living in stockaded towns set on terraces above rivers. On their broad fertile fields they raised corn, beans, and squash and a plant new to de Soto called tobacco. The Indian houses were made of wattle and daub and their roofs were thatched. De Soto was impressed by how much they looked like the typical European villages he knew, except that the Indian villages were much cleaner. At the east end of each town was a temple raised on a pyramid of earth.

These Indians—the Choctaw, Chickasaw, Natchez, Biloxi—were skilled in basketry and pottery, and they carved in wood, bone, shell, and semi-precious stones. Some were traders who canoed inland north and south on the rivers to exchange home goods for those made by other peoples.

Although they were peaceful, the Indians de Soto met did not welcome invaders who looted the treasures of their temples and tortured and killed anyone who opposed them. But bow and arrow could not defeat firearms, and most towns gave up resistance and waited for the hated strangers to move on.

West and north de Soto advanced, reaching the lands of the Creek nations. They spoke the Muskogee tongue, like the Choctaw and Chickasaw. And their material mode of life—towns, temples, and agriculture—was similar too. English traders later divided them into the

Upper and Lower Creeks according to the regions they lived in. There were certain differences between the two groups, but they shared the same basic pattern of culture.

Their population of forty thousand lived in some fifty towns scattered throughout Georgia, Alabama, and their fringes. The Creeks set their villages close by a river, stream, or spring. They raised corn, melons, beans, and pumpkins, and when the soil wore out, moved to another place. They farmed and hunted to feed themselves, and in this period when the whites first knew them did not try to raise a surplus for trading. Their hunting territory was tribally owned.

Each Creek town, averaging about eight hundred persons, governed itself. Its headman or chief had power but seldom used it without consulting with the town council. Often every man in the tribe was present when a major decision was to be made. The men of a town who had proved their standing chose the chief and confined the post to one family line so long as it produced effective leaders. The town council could impeach a chief any time he was considered unsatisfactory.

The chief's duties were many. He was in charge of the public granary, where some of the harvest from the town's fields was stored. After a successful hunt he invited the town to a feast that concluded with an all-night dance. He chaired discussions at the town council, steering them to a decision. He picked the time for the annual harvest ceremony, received embassies from other towns and tribes, and spoke for his town in dealings with the world outside.

Among the town council was a group that directed the planting, cultivating, and harvesting of the town fields, and the collecting of leaves for the "black drink," the emetic and purge used at all ceremonies.

Home to a Creek man (and later to the Seminole) was where the women of his mother's clan lived. Thus, the chiefs were chosen from the hereditary line of the women. Prowess in war was what started a Creek up the ladder of office. Once he was on the lower rungs, his ability as an orator or administrator and his knowledge of tribal law and lore could send him on to the highest positions in leadership in the Creek culture. A man showed his rank by painting his face and body in prescribed patterns.

While each Creek town was separate and independent, a loose confederacy grew up among them. With the coming of the Europeans, it became tighter and more influential. The towns came together usually once a year, in May, for a council meeting that hundreds of delegates and thousands of tribesmen attended. They took up political issues but gave ample time to ceremony and recreation, too. No king or leader held absolute power in the confederacy. By thorough discussion, in a kind of participatory democracy, the Creeks tried to find unity. They knew they could protect themselves best by pooling their warrior power. Still, each town remained free to fight or make peace.

James Adair, an educated Scotsman who lived for

almost fifty years among the Southeastern Indians, said the Creeks breathed nothing but liberty.

The warlike ways of the Creeks gave de Soto trouble. They fought hard to defend their lands. They ran off Spanish horses and cattle, stole and ate the Spaniards' sheep and pigs, and killed their hunting dogs. De Soto soon pushed north into the Cherokee country.

It is not easy to trace how the Seminole Indians emerged from the Creek. The Seminole were not a tribe in the usual sense. They were a composite of many small groups of Indians, the remnants of tribes and bands. When Creeks began drifting into Florida in the first years of the eighteenth century, the original tribes of Florida were almost extinct. The newcomers established a few villages, which gradually lost their Creek identity. They made raids against the Spaniards and their Indian allies and learned much about the Florida wilderness.

Their numbers were increased in 1715 when several groups of Indians warred against the English colonists in South Carolina because these frontier traders had cheated and abused them. When the Indians lost, some retreated far south to St. Augustine and settled nearby.

From 1750 to about 1812, half a dozen villages took root in the northern part of Florida. From that base, Indian hunters roved the peninsula for bear, deer, and the cattle running wild from ranches the Spanish had given up.

Florida was rich not only in fish and game but in a wide variety of berries, fruits, and vegetables. Indians who wished to put plenty of space between themselves and the white man could find ample food here.

Some bands of Lower Creek moved south because white settlers were crowding them in Georgia and the herds of deer were shrinking. Encountering one of these bands, the Oconee, William Bartram learned what prompted their migration. They needed to move constantly because the maize and beans they grew exhausted the soil rapidly. But whenever they looked for more fertile land, they risked battle with the hostile tribes surrounding them. In Florida they hoped to find a place uninhabited by other Indians. Settling in the Alachua region, this group became the nucleus for the principal Seminole tribe.

3

Band of Brotherhood

How the Seminole lived was recorded by William Bartram. A trained natural scientist from Philadelphia, he traveled through the South in the mid-1770's, noting down everything he saw. Welcomed by the Alachua tribe, he wrote this description of where they lived:

> The town of Cuscowilla, which is the capital of the Alachua tribe, contains about thirty habitations, each of which consists of two houses nearly the same size, about thirty feet in length, twelve feet wide, and about the same in height. The door is placed midway on one side or in the front. This house is divided equally, across, into two apartments, one of which is the cook room and common hall, and the other the lodging room. The other house is nearly of the same dimensions, standing about twenty yards from the dwelling house, its end fronting the door. The building is two stories high, and constructed in a different manner. It is

divided transversely, as the other, but the end next the dwelling house is open on three sides, supported by posts or pillars. It has an open loft or platform, the ascent to which is by a portable stair or ladder: this is a pleasant, cool, airy situation, and here the master or chief of the family retires to repose in the hot seasons, and receives his guests or visitors. The other half of this building is closed on all sides by notched logs; the lowest or ground part is a potato house, and the upper story over it a granary for corn and other provisions.

Their houses are constructed of a kind of frame. In the first place, strong corner pillars are fixed in the ground, with others somewhat less, ranging on a line between; these are strengthened by cross pieces of timber, and the whole with the roof is covered close with the bark of the cypress tree. The dwelling stands near the middle of a square yard, encompassed by a low bank, formed with the earth taken out of the yard, which is always carefully swept. Their towns are clean, the inhabitants being particular in laying their filth at a proper distance from their dwellings, which undoubtedly contributes to the healthiness of their habitations.

The setting the Seminole chose for their town pleased Bartram:

The town stands on the most pleasant situation that could be well imagined or desired, in an inland country; upon a high swelling ridge of sand hills, within three or four hundred yards of a large and beautiful lake, the circular shore of which continually washes a sandy beach, under a moderately high sloping bank, terminated on one side by extensive forests, consisting of orange groves, overtopped with grand magnolias, palms, poplar, tilia, live oaks, and others. . . . The opposite point of the crescent gradually retires with hummocky projecting points, indenting the grassy marshes, and lastly terminates in infinite green plains and meadows, united with the skies and waters of the lake. Such a natural landscape, such a rural scene, is not to be imitated by the united ingenuity and labor of man. At present the ground betwixt the town and the lake is adorned by an open grove of very tall pine trees, which standing at a considerable distance from each other, admit a delightful prospect of the sparkling waters. The lake abounds with various excellent fish and wild fowl. There are incredible numbers of the latter, especially in the winter season, when they arrive here from the north to winter.

The Seminole used primitive stone tools to cultivate their land until they bought iron axes and hoes from white traders. They had horses (originally brought by the Spanish) but never developed farm implements that could be harnessed to horse power. Bartram describes their farming:

They plant but little here about the town; only a small garden plot at each habitation, consisting of a little corn, beans, tobacco, citruls, etc. Their plantation, which supplies them with the chief of their vegetable provisions . . . lies on the rich prolific lands bordering on the great Alachua savanna, about two miles distance.

This plantation is one common enclosure, and is worked and tended by the whole community; yet every family has its particular part. . . .

The youth, under the supervision of some of their ancient people, are daily stationed in the fields, and are continually whooping and hallooing, to chase away crows, jackdaws, blackbirds, and such predatory animals; and the lads are armed with bows and arrows, and being trained up to it from their early youth, are sure at a mark, and in the course of the day load themselves with squirrels, birds, etc. The men in turn patrol the corn fields at night, to protect their provisions from the depredations of night rovers, as bears, raccoons, and deer; the two former being immoderately fond of young corn, when the grain is filled with a rich milk, as sweet and nourishing as cream; and the deer are as fond of the potato vines.

Their communal method of farming is worth more notice. Bartram was impressed by it and gives us these details:

The whole town plant in one vast field together; but yet the part or share of every individual family or habitation is separated from the next adjoining by a narrow strip, or verge of grass, or any other natural or artificial boundary.

In the spring, the ground being already prepared on one and the same day, early in the morning, the whole town is summoned by the sound of a conch shell, from the mouth of the overseer, to meet at the public square, whither the people repair with their hoes and axes, and from thence proceed to their plantation, where they begin to plant, not every one in his own little district, assigned and laid out, but the whole community united begins on one certain part of the field, where they plant on until finished; and when their rising crops are ready for dressing and cleansing they proceed after the same order, and so on day after day, until the crop is laid by for ripening.

After the feast of the husk [the Green Corn Dance] is over, and all the grain is ripe, the whole town again assemble, and every man carries off the fruits of his labor, from the part first allotted to him, which he deposits in his own granary, which is individually his own.

But previous to their carrying off their crops from the field, there is a large crib or granary, erected in the plantation, which is called the king's crib. To this each family carries and deposits a certain quantity, according to his ability or inclination, or none at all if he so chooses. This in appearance seems a tribute or revenue to the micco. But in fact is designed for another purpose, that of a public treasury . . . to which every citizen has the right of free and equal access when his own private stores are consumed. [The treasury also serves] as a surplus to fly to for succor, to assist neighboring towns whose crops may have failed, accommodate strangers or travellers, afford provisions or supplies when they go forth on hostile expeditions, and for all other exigencies of the state. And this treasure is at the disposal of the king or micco, which is surely a royal attribute, to have an exclusive right and ability in a community to distribute comfort and blessings to the necessitous.

Several plants native to Florida, Bartram saw, were important to the Seminole. Koonti, a starch, was grated and sieved and made into a cake or boiled to a soft gruel called soffkee.

The Seminole raised what they called a "hanging pumpkin." It was planted at the butt of a dead tree, and the vines climbed up and out onto the branches. It was a kind of vertical agriculture that kept the fruit safe from pigs and cattle and saved ground space, too. The greenish pumpkin is small and so hard it sometimes has to be cut open with an ax, like a coconut. Its superior flavor made it a favorite food, important in the Seminole diet. Cut in strips and dried, it could be stored for use in time of food shortage.

The guava, a fruit, had a flavor like the strawberry. Its seeds could be roasted, ground, or mixed with the pulp to make a guava cheese. The fresh fruit yielded three times its weight in jelly. Scientists discovered later that the guava is one of the richest of all fruits in vitamins.

A bitter bark called Florida quinine came from a small tree that grew in the swamp. It is related to the cinchona tree of South America that supplies the quinine to control intermittent fevers such as malaria, and seems to contain the same curative element. The Seminole used it as a medicine.

From another plant came the "black drink," central to the ceremony of the Green Corn Dance and other festivities that called for purification. It is an emetic holly, *Ilex vomitoria.* The Indian name for the plant is "asi." An evergreen tree, it grows to twelve or fifteen feet in moist, shady places. Many Southern tribes regarded it as a holy plant. They boiled the strong tealike potion and filled gourds with it to use during religious rites or at council meetings. It cleared the stomach thoroughly. In the ritual that preceded a war party, the men had to purify themselves in the black-drink ceremony. The warriors sat in a circle. When all were ready to drink, they gave the long-drawn-out cry, "Asi-yahola," and took the potion from a medicine man. Then from time to time each man cleared his insides in a spout that shot six to eight feet in the air. After the ceremony, the warriors fasted. The Seminole believed the black drink gave them skill and courage in war.

Hunting balanced farming among the Seminole. In Florida the deer were so plentiful that they became the chief source of meat and hides and the principal product for trade. But by 1750, armed with the white man's musket, the Seminole had almost destroyed the herds. They shifted then to raising cattle, beginning with the wild herds the Spanish rancheros had abandoned. Cattle-raising became not a communal but a private occupation. The herds were owned by individuals. After a time the size of a man's herd gave him standing, just as valor in war did. The land, however, remained the group's. No individual could own it.

The Seminole economy was mixed then: part private and part communal. It led to differences in wealth and position. One man might be rich enough to sell a thousand head of cattle a year from his own herds. Students of the Seminole think that the idea of personal gain grew out of association with the white man. Whites who dealt with the Indians, whether as private traders or as government agents, often tried hard to break down their communal ways.

The name "Seminole" was first used in 1771 by an Englishman, John Stuart, an Indian agent. The word has been given several meanings, all somewhat related. To Stuart it meant "wild people," because these Indian bands liked to live apart, by themselves. To other whites it meant "runaways." The Indians identified as Seminole speak of themselves as "the people of the peninsula."

White Americans came to use the word to refer to all those tribes or groups who moved into upper Florida. When larger groups formed out of smaller ones came to their attention, whites had to put a label on them. Such fusions of peoples went on all the time in that period.

At first, "Seminole" meant only the Alachua band and its many offshoots. By 1810 it encompassed all Florida Indians, whether they spoke Muskogee or Hitchiti.

From the Muskogee tongue came the words the Seminole used for titles of war and peace. "Micco" meant chief or peace leader; "tustenugee," war leader; "micanopy," topmost king. Then there was "emathla" for the leader of a band who had proved himself in war, "heneka" for lieutenant, "hillis haya" for the principal medicine man. Honors earned in battle brought the title of "hadjo" for reckless courage and "fixico" for fearless conduct. The Seminole kept his baby name until he had earned a title for prowess in war. After that his given name was never used, and the earned name was the name he became known by in history.

Listening to the Seminole speak Muskogee, Bartram said of it:

> This language is very agreeable to the ear, courteous, gentle, and musical: the letter R is not sounded in one word of their language. The women in particular speak so fine and musical, as to repre-

sent the singing of birds; and when heard and not seen, one might imagine it to be the prattling of young children. The men's speech is indeed more strong and sonorous, but not harsh, and in no instance guttural. . . .

All the Indian languages are truly rhetorical, or figurative, assisting their speech by tropes; their hands, fixture of the head, the brow, in short, every member, naturally associate, and give their assistance to render their harangues eloquent, persuasive and effectual.

What did the Seminole look like? Bartram describes the men and women:

The males are tall, erect, and moderately robust; their limbs well shaped, so as generally to form a perfect human figure; their features regular, and countenance open, dignified and placid; yet the forehead and brow so formed, as to strike you instantly with heroism and bravery; the eye though rather small, yet active and full of fire; the iris always black, and the nose commonly inclining to the aquiline.

Their countenance and actions exhibit an air of magnanimity, superiority and independence.

Their complexion of a reddish brown or copper colour; their hair long, lank, coarse, and black as a raven, and reflecting the like luster at different exposures to the light.

The women, though remarkably short of stature,

are well formed; their visage round, features regular and beautiful; and brow high and arched; the eye large, black, and languishing, expressive of modesty, diffidence, and bashfulness; these charms are their defensive and offensive weapons, and they know very well how to play them off, and under cover of these alluring graces, are concealed the most subtle artifice; they are, however, loving and affectionate.

As for the character of the Seminole Indians, Bartram had this to say:

A proud, haughty and arrogant race of men; they are brave and valiant in war, ambitious of conquest, restless and perpetually exercising their arms, yet magnanimous and merciful to a vanquished enemy, when he submits and seeks their friendship and protection: always uniting the vanquished tribes in confederacy with them; when they immediately enjoy, unexceptionally, every right of free citizens, and are from that moment united in one common band of brotherhood. . . .

If we consider them with respect to their private character in a moral view, they must, I think, claim our approbation, if we divest ourselves of prejudice and think freely. As moral men they certainly stand in no need of European civilization.

They are just, honest, liberal, and hospitable to strangers; considerate, loving and affectionate to their wives and relations; fond of their children; industrious, frugal, temperate and persevering; charitable and forbearing. I have been weeks and months amongst them and in their towns, and never observed the least sign of contention or wrangling: never saw an instance of an Indian beating his wife, or even reproving her in anger. In this case they stand as examples of reproof to the most civilized nations, as not being defective in justice, gratitude, and a good understanding; for indeed their wives merit their esteem and the most gentle treatment, they being industrious, frugal, careful, loving and affectionate.

Bartram goes on to give us an interesting glimpse of their social behavior:

A man goes forth on his business or avocation; he calls in at another town; if he wants victuals, rest or social conversation, he confidently approaches the door of the first house he chooses, saying "I am come." The good man or woman replies, "You are; it's well." Immediately victuals and drink are ready; he eats and drinks a little, then smokes tobacco, and converses either of private matters, public talks, or the news of the town. He rises and says, "I go!" the other answers, "You do!" He then proceeds again, and steps in at the next habitation he likes, or repairs to the public square, where are people always conversing by day, or dancing at night, or to some more private assembly, as he likes. He needs no one to introduce him, any more than the blackbird or thrush. . . .

The Green Corn Dance was the greatest ceremony of the year for the Seminole. It came from Creek ritual and was held when the corn was in the roasting-ear stage—July or August. It was a New Year's rite to regenerate the world and all the plants, animals, and people who dwelt on it. The ritual lasted four days usually, though sometimes it was repeated for another four. Each town celebrated this husk, or feast of first fruits, when its own harvest was ready.

The supreme deity had taught the Indians the ceremony, it was believed. The chief roles were played by the top-ranking medicine men. They made the new fire and brewed the black drink. The supreme deity lived in the sky and was linked to, but not identical with, the sun. On earth he was represented by the sacred fire.

On the first day, the town square was cleared and arranged and a new fire started. The second day, the people feasted on new corn. On the third, all the mature men fasted and then took the emetic, the black drink. The fourth day, the town feasted on venison seasoned with salt and on the new corn and fruits, brought from the harvest fold. The young men played ball games, and then the whole night long everyone danced, sang, and rejoiced. For the entire four days, said Bartram, "they abstain from the gratification of every appetite and passion whatever."

The New Year was marked by the making of new clothing, pots, pans, furniture, tools, and weapons; the old things were tossed on a common heap and burned. The houses, squares, the whole town, were swept and cleaned. Every Seminole household put out the fire on the first day and renewed it on the fourth, using the new drill made on the first day.

The most significant aspect of the Green Corn ceremony was the forgiving of every wrong, short of murder. Sometimes those who had done wrong hid in the woods until the time of the great ceremony. Then they came back to their villages to be forgiven and restored to full citizenship. In terms of moral life, it was a fresh beginning.

While this restoration of internal peace was vital, the Green Corn Dance was also the occasion for propitiating animal spirits to insure better hunting. Nor was the war-maker neglected. The warriors slept on graded bed platforms in the town square and were granted new names and ranks for distinction in battles of the past year.

This was a happy people. There was no doubt of it in Bartram's eyes:

This handful of people possesses a vast territory—all East Florida and the greatest part of West Florida, which being naturally cut and divided into thousands of islets, knolls and eminences, by the innumerable rivers, lakes, swamps, vast savannas and ponds, form so many secure retreats and temporary dwelling places, that effectually guard them from any sudden invasions or attacks from their enemies; and being such a swampy, hummocky country, furnishes such a plenty and variety of supplies for the nourishment of varieties of animals, that I can venture to assert that no part of the globe so abounds with wild game or creatures fit for the food of man.

Thus they enjoy a superabundance of the necessaries and conveniences of life, with the security of person and property, the two great concerns of mankind. The hides of deer, bears, tigers and wolves, together with honey, wax and other productions of the country, purchase their clothing, equipage, and domestic utensils from the whites. They seem to be free from want or desires. No cruel enemy to dread, nothing to give them disquietude, but the gradual encroachments of the white people. Thus contented and undisturbed, they appear as blithe and free as the birds of the air, and like them as volatile and active, tuneful and vociferous.

The visage, action, and deportment of the Seminole form the most striking picture of happiness in this life. Joy, contentment, love, and friendship, without guile or affectation, seem inherent in them or predominant in their vital principle, for it leaves them but with the last breath of life. . . .

4

Black Fugitives

"Nothing to give them disquietude, but the gradual encroachments of the white people . . ."

What Bartram saw as only a faint threat to the Seminole would become, within a few years, a terrible menace.

The American Revolution, fought in the name of independence, freedom, and equality, birthed a new nation that would allow the Indians none of those rights. Almost at once, the citizens of the United States showed they would not live peaceably side by side with Indians on their southern border—or Indians anywhere.

Until this time, no one European nation had succeeded in taking control of the region that became the United States. As the white people struggled among themselves, most of the Indians managed to remain independent. Probably they thought the Europeans would reach some kind of balance of power that would not threaten their own existence. By the end of the

American Revolution, only a few small Indian tribes, along the east coast, where white settlement was heaviest, had gone under. Almost everywhere else, from the Atlantic to the Mississippi, the Indian nations kept themselves intact in the face of the white threat.

Meanwhile, the Indians, widely diverse among themselves, discovered, in the common arena where they met, how diverse the European invaders were. In speech, in dress, in tools, in the ways they carried on trade, religious ceremonies, politics, diplomacy, war. By the end of the 1700's the Indians east of the Mississippi began to realize that not only their homelands but their way of life were endangered.

The goods which the traders introduced bred new habits and ways of living. By 1670 the Southeastern Indians were using glass beads, hatchets, hoes, adzes, and knives. Close by the English settlements were Indians who already dressed in hats, shoes, stockings, breeches, and linen shirts. By 1715 a coarse cloth was the staple of the trade, made up into vivid red or blue blankets. The Indians used the whites' axes and broad hoes to clear and cultivate their fields. They traded for brass kettles, knives, flints, and guns with powder and bullets for war and the hunt. For the Indian women there were needles, thread, scissors, petticoats, flowered calico, and lace. And for the men, besides the linen shirts, there were laced coats, and hats, and even small mirrors.

"The Indian trade," wrote the influential American historian, Frederick Jackson Turner, "pioneered the way for civilization. . . ." He called it a "progress from savage conditions. . . ." But Turner, like so many others before and after him, did not see the exploitation of the American continent from the Indian's point of view. The traders created a demand for merchandise the Indians did not make, or put the native industries out of business. Then, whenever the whites wanted to bring a troublesome tribe to terms, they would threaten to cut off trade. Guns and bullets became the most important articles of trade. And the whites bluntly used that fact as a threat.

To whip the Creeks into line in 1725, the English agent Tobias Fitch made this speech to them:

> I must tell your young men that had it not been for us they would not have known how to war nor yet have anything to war with. For before we came among you, there was no other weapons than bows and arrows to hunt with. You could hunt a whole day and bring nothing home at night. You had no other hoes or axes than stones. You wore nothing but skins. But now we have learned you the use of firearms, as well to kill deer, and other provisions, as to war against your enemies. This you that are old men know to be true, and I would have you make your young men sensible of it.

You cannot live without us now, he was telling them.

But living with the whites and their ways meant the early rape of the land. The traders and frontiersmen were often ruthlessly destructive in their greed for profit. From the 1730's on, they shipped over 160,000 deerskins a year from Georgia and South Carolina alone. It was an enormous slaughter of deer. It compares in its terrible waste with what a later generation did to the buffalo of the Great Plains.

The white traders dealt in human animals too. The traffic in Indian slaves was an important part of the business until the early eighteenth century. The whites set one Indian people against another to take slaves. At English prodding, the Chickasaw captured five hundred Choctaw and killed three times that number in less than a decade.

Although many Indian slaves were put to work in the colonies, the general policy was to export them, for Indian slaves would flee to the forests and the white settlers feared they would conspire with other tribes to rise against them. It was safer to ship the red slaves to New England or the West Indies.

Of course, there was a ready argument to justify the Indian slave trade: "Some men think," wrote the Carolinian Captain Nairne, "that it both serves to lessen their numbers before the French can arm them, and it is a more effectual way of civilizing and instructing [them] than all the efforts used by the French missionaries."

Contact with the whites led to an important change in Indian politics, too. Many groups of Indians made alliances—among themselves, or with one or another of the European nations. Such alliances were used for both offense and defense. Sometimes it helped the Indians to survive; sometimes not.

In the end, the Americans emerged from among the white invaders as the dominant power. First the British had eliminated the French, in a struggle called the French and Indian Wars. Then the Americans (as the British colonials were called) broke free of the mother country.

Except for a brief twenty years when the British held it, Florida in all this time was in the control of the Spanish. But Spain was too weak a power now to do harm to the Indians. The Spanish clung only to a few small settlements on the coast of the peninsula, and the Indians lived much as they liked. More and more Creeks moved across the border into Florida, fleeing before the appetite of the landless whites, who gnawed voraciously at Indian hunting grounds and fields. To all who came—red or black—the Spanish gave freedom and citizenship.

That was where the trouble started.

For living among the Seminole were black people—none the less Seminole for being black. Many were runaway slaves who, like the Indians, had long before begun the move down into Florida in search of a free life.

As early as 1704, a Spanish governor had opened Florida to fugitives from British plantations to the north. He armed them and treated them as free men. That liberty was a magnet to the Carolina slaves. They ran off to St. Augustine and settled north of the town. The fugitives were numerous enough for the Spanish to form them into black regiments and garrison them in a strategically located black fort. Their former white masters often found themselves fighting against ex-slaves, who, in alliance with Indians, raided the South Carolina and Georgia frontiers.

The Spanish looked to their buffer settlements of red and black allies to hold the Florida border against the English. Eventually England and Spain went to war. When England took Havana, Spain gave up Florida to get back her Cuban port. The blacks of St. Augustine were transferred to Cuba.

But in the remoter western parts of Florida, blacks kept moving in along with the Creek Indians. And when Spain got Florida back in 1783, in exchange for the Bahamas, the tide of runaway slaves rolled in higher and higher.

The blacks in Florida were now of two groups—one free, and the other legally slaves of the Seminole. The enslavement of blacks by the Indians had developed in the Southern colonies by 1750. The Five Civilized Tribes, as they were called (the Cherokees, Chickasaws, Choctaws, Creeks, and the Seminole who seceded from the Creeks), became slaveholders just as their white neighbors had, and for some of the same reasons.

Among the tribes, slavery took different forms. And attitudes to slavery varied from person to person within a tribe. The Cherokees, who took up white ways more than the others, adopted much the same kind of slavery as the whites, though they were more lenient to the blacks. The Choctaw and Chickasaw are said to have been "great sticklers for racial purity." The Creeks showed no racial prejudice and treated the slaves in the patriarchal manner of the Old Testament Hebrews. "They took slave women for their handmaids," says the historian Kenneth W. Porter, "and brought up the children they had by them on a practical equality with their full-blooded offspring." "In no other tribe," Porter goes on, "was the Negro's position higher than among the Seminoles."

It was in the time of British control of Florida and the turmoil of the American Revolution that blacks became slaves of the Creeks and the Seminole. Indian leaders saw the prestige slave-owning gave the whites and some were moved to exchange cattle, hogs, or horses for blacks. The British also made gifts of blacks to Creek chiefs to reward them for their services in the Revolution. Other blacks were taken prisoner during the Revolution or in sporadic raids on plantations.

Slavery under the Seminole was so different from what it was under the whites that everyone who observed it thought it important to record the fact. John Lee Williams wrote that in 1834 the Seminole's slaves

> live in villages separate, and, in many cases, remote from their own, and enjoying equal liberty with their owners, with the single exception that the slave supplies his owner annually, from the product of his little field, with corn, in proportion to the

> amount of the crop; and in no case that has come to my knowledge, exceeding ten bushels; the residue is considered the property of the slave. Many of these slaves have stocks of horses, cows, and hogs, with which the Indian owner never assumes the right to intermeddle.

Given so high a degree of freedom and responsibility, the Seminole's blacks prospered. An American surveyor working near them in 1822 described them as "stout and even gigantic in their proportions . . . the finest looking people I have ever seen."

Such news traveled fast along the black grapevine. Slaves on the border regions fled south to place themselves under the protection of the Seminole chiefs. They paid in return a small tribute of grain or livestock. They built homes in their own villages, tilled the soil, raised livestock, hunted, and fished. They dressed the way the Seminole did—stripped down for work, and on festive occasions adorned themselves splendidly in turbans and shawls, smocks, moccasins, leggings, and metal ornaments. The men carried guns, and in battle served under their own black captains. Since no racial bars were raised against them, intermarriage was common. Those who knew English or Spanish as well as the Seminole tongue became interpreters or spies. Many blacks, wise in their understanding of the white man's ways, became valued advisors. They were fully trusted by the Seminole in both war and council.

them together. Together they stood a better chance of resisting the white enemy. Having even more to lose, the black warriors fought as hard or harder than the Indians.

The free blacks allied to the Seminole were runaway slaves who had made good their freedom. (Sometimes they were called maroons, after the Spanish word for that condition.) Among them were recent fugitives certain to be reclaimed by their masters if any white authority could lay hands on them, as well as blacks, born among the Seminole, who were the descendants of runaway slaves. The blacks born among the Seminole were still legally the slaves of the whites from whom their parents had fled, or of the heirs of those slaveholders. They too could (and would) be reclaimed, even though identification was now impossible.

Just how many blacks there were among the Florida Indians is very hard to say. Joshua Giddings, who wrote *The Exiles of Florida,* an authoritative book about them, estimated that in 1836 there were fourteen hundred black people living among the Seminole. About two hundred were slaves, he said.

Here, then, was the root of the conflict that led to America's longest, bloodiest, and most costly Indian war. On the one side, whites greedy for land and the slaves to work that land. On the other side, Indians who had the land and sheltered the runaway slaves—and would not give them up.

5

It "Belongs" to Us

As the price of slaves went up, every runaway slave became an even more painful loss to the planters. The newly invented cotton gin, making production more profitable and spreading plantations everywhere, was one cause of higher slave prices. Another was the 1808 law which banned the importation of slaves into the United States. Planters would try every means, legal or illegal, to get the slave labor they needed.

South of Georgia was Florida, a haven for fugitive slaves. The fact that Florida was foreign territory, belonging to Spain, did not bother the planters. They raided across the border time and again to take black captives. They were only claiming their own runaways, they said—but any black was fair game.

With the supply of slaves from outside the United States legally cut off, the whites turned to bootlegging labor. Florida, with its long, thinly settled coastline and its nearness to Cuba, became an ideal base for slave-smugglers. Black flesh priced at a dollar a pound now brought $300 to $400 delivered from Florida. Slave ships from the Caribbean sailed their black cargoes up Florida waterways, where agents took them over and sneaked them across the border to American plantations. But many a night the smugglers were ambushed by Seminole reds and blacks and the slaves set free.

Charges flew back and forth. The Georgians accused the Seminole of stealing their slaves, and the Seminole accused the Georgians of raiding their borders to kidnap the blacks.

Anxious to get their hands on both the Florida lands and the Florida blacks, whites in the border region plotted to take the peninsula from Spain. Florida belongs to us, they said, the way a foot belongs to a leg. We have a "right" to take it.

That reasoning is worth a close look.

What the American settlers wanted was Florida's land and the labor to work it. Hard, practical goals. But in that drive for selfish interests, they needed the support of others: the government, of course, and if it came to war, the people who would do the fighting. No one would fight for another's personal gain. The way the land-hungry people could win support was to appeal to emotion, to give a moral tone to their material interests.

Masses of men will respond to a moral appeal. Tell them they must act to vindicate a right or correct a wrong and they will move. That is the way governments—American as well as others—have sought to keep their people behind them, whether their policy was right or wrong.

Most people do have a sense of morality, a conscience. But conscience can be played upon by men for the most questionable motives. And in a nation's politics the moral argument almost never leads to giving up something, but rather to acquiring something.

American morality was founded on the idea of inalienable natural rights—"the right to life, liberty, and the pursuit of happiness." And the right to self-determination—which meant we could break away from Great Britain to govern ourselves.

We thought of ourselves, too, as the special champions of the rights of *all* men. Tom Paine said it—America's cause is "the cause of all mankind." That came to mean we had a national mission. We would extend our influence to "savage, enslaved and benighted nations."

But not by conquest. That would interfere with other people's natural right to self-determination. And what basis does conquest have but the law of the strongest? That is no moral basis at all.

Yet here were the white settlers sitting on the edge of the American continent, and hungry for all that vast land stretching away before their eyes. Almost at once they began talking about getting some of that land. Not to satisfy greed! Only to fend off dangerous neighbors —the Indians, of course, and the Europeans competing for that same land. Soon it appeared to the new Americans that their future security was superior to anyone else's interests. We not only had a "natural right" to liberty; we had a "natural right" to security and safety.

It sounded good and proper, until you stopped to ask: What makes for security? What practical steps are permissible to attain security? Who defines it? Who draws the line? The right of security proved to be a very convenient excuse for expanding whenever and wherever we liked. Canada on the north, the Western lands beyond the Alleghenies, Florida to the south . . . it seemed we needed them all. It was only "what the Deity intended for us," as one American said. Such reliance on God's will gave us an unshakable moral confidence when we thought of expansion and the aggression that usually went with it.

Our objective soon became to control the North American continent. The very geography of the continent, some were saying, gave us Americans a "manifest destiny." That is, we had a natural right to all the territory needed for our security. And that right must override the rights claimed by the people already living in that territory. Jefferson had once said, "Every man and every body of men on earth possesses the right of self-government." But not, it seems, when that right conflicted with the rights of Americans.

Under Jefferson we doubled our land by the purchase from Napoleon of the Louisiana Territory. But the appetite for land grew by what it fed upon. "Since the

Americans have acquired Louisiana," wrote a Frenchman in 1814, "they appear to be unable to bear any barriers around them."

In no time, we were pursuing Florida with a passion. "Nature," said Governor William Claiborne, "has decreed the union of Florida with the United States." To Senator Gouverneur Morris, too, Florida was "a natural and necessary part of our empire." Senator Andrew Jackson was confident that "God and nature have destined New Orleans and the Floridas to belong to this great and rising empire." Senator Henry Clay's sense of beauty led him to declare that Florida was desirable because "it fills a space in our imagination."

Besides, as many pointed out, Florida was located right next to us. It was a "natural appendage" of the United States. Anything touching our borders, then, belonged to us—a doctrine widely used to claim territory. But where do you stop? As soon as you take over one piece of land, you come up against another (if not a body of water). And that land, too, belongs to you.

So the notion that Florida naturally belonged to the United States gave moral force to those who wanted to expand south. The finger of God was pointing in just the direction the Georgians and others wanted to move.

Anything that would speed that move, the whites were willing to try. General Mathews of Georgia put out feelers to see if bribery of a Spanish governor would not deliver East Florida to the United States. When that failed, Mathews cooked up an "uprising."

He wanted to make it appear that the people living under Spanish rule were rebelling spontaneously.

That plot failed, too, for the Spanish colonials did not relish American domination, and the blacks and the Seminole had their own good reasons to unite against the threat. Georgia militia marched one hundred miles into Florida to try to crush the Alachua towns of the Seminole. For two weeks the Indians conducted a running fight with the whites and almost wiped them out.

That defeat only spurred the whites to try harder. A few months later, Tennessee volunteers joined by United States regulars ripped into northern Florida. "Every Negro taken in arms will be put to death," said the commander. His men burned about four hundred Indian homes, destroyed stores of food, and stole hundreds of horses and cattle. But they failed to capture a single black. Seminole resistance had stopped this attempt to annex Florida to the United States.

Knowing well the white man's ambitions, Tecumseh, the great Shawnee leader, tried to weld an alliance of many tribes to resist the Americans. In 1812 he came south and made this plea to a Choctaw and Chickasaw council:

> The whites are already nearly a match for us all united, and too strong for any one tribe alone to resist; so that unless we support one another with our collective and united forces, unless every tribe unanimously combines to give a check to the am-

bition and avarice of the whites, they will soon conquer us apart and disunited, and we will be driven away from our native country and scattered as autumnal leaves before the wind. . . .

Our broad domains are fast escaping from our grasp. Every year our white intruders become more greedy, exacting, oppressive, and overbearing. Every year contentions spring up between them and our people and when blood is shed we have to make atonement whether right or wrong, at the cost of the lives of our greatest chiefs, and the yielding up of large tracts of our lands. Before the pale-faces came among us we enjoyed the happiness of unbounded freedom, and were acquainted with neither riches, wants nor oppression.

How is it now? Wants and oppressions are our lot; for are we not controlled in everything, and dare we move without asking, by your leave? Are we not being stripped day by day of the little that remains of our ancient liberty? Do they not even now kick and strike us as they do their black-faces? How long will it be before they will tie us to a post and whip us and make us work for them in cornfields as they do them? Shall we wait for that moment or shall we die fighting before submitting to such ignominy? . . .

War or extermination is now our only choice. Which do you choose . . . to assist in the just cause of liberating our race from the grasp of our faithless invaders and heartless oppressors. The

> white usurpation in our common country must be stopped or we, the rightful owners, be forever destroyed and wiped out as a race of people. . . .

Tecumseh's call for armed resistance was answered by the Choctaw orator, Pushmataha. He argued that the Indians should not fight, but work out ways of living with the whites:

> What people, my friends and countrymen, were so unwise and inconsiderate as to engage in a war of their own accord, when their own strength, and even the aid of others, was judged unequal to the task? I well know, causes often arise which force men to confront extremities, but my countrymen, those causes do not now exist. . . . You now have no just cause to declare war against the American people, or wreak your vengeance upon them as enemies, since they have ever manifested feelings of friendship toward you. . . .
>
> The war, which you are now contemplating against the Americans, is a flagrant breach of justice; yea, a fearful blemish on your honor and also that of your fathers, and which you will find if you will examine it carefully and judiciously, forbodes nothing but destruction to our entire race. It is a war against a people whose territories are now far greater than our own, and who are far better provided with all necessary implements of war, with men, guns, horses, wealth, far beyond that of all our race combined, and where is the necessity or

wisdom to make war upon such a people? Where is our hope of success, if thus weak and unprepared we should declare it against them?

Let us not be deluded with the foolish hope that this war, if begun, will soon be over, even if we destroy all the whites within our territories, and lay waste their homes and fields. Far from it. It will be but the beginning of the end that terminates in the total destruction of our race. And though we will not permit ourselves to be made slaves, or, like inexperienced warriors, shudder at the thought of war, yet I am not so insensible and incсnsistent as to advise you to cowardly yield to the outrages of the whites, or wilfully to connive at their unjust encroachments; but only not yet to have recourse to war, but to send ambassadors to our Great Father at Washington, and lay before him our grievances, without betraying too great eagerness for war, or manifesting any tokens of pusillanimity. . . .

I implore you, while healing measures are in the election of us all, not to break the treaty nor violate your pledge or honor, but to submit our grievances, whatever they may be, to the Congress of the United States, according to the articles of the treaty existing between us and the American people. . . .

The Choctaws and the Chickasaws took Pushmataha's advice. But not the Seminole. They listened to Tecumseh when he visited them in Florida. Like him, they were convinced that the Indians had to fight to survive.

When the conflict between the British and the Americans broke out in the War of 1812, Tecumseh joined the British side. The Creeks split over Tecumseh's policy. The Lower Creeks stood for peace with the Americans. The Upper, more hostile to the whites, followed Tecumseh's teaching. They were called the Red Sticks. They rose against the Americans all along the frontier.

For a time the Red Sticks more than held their own. Then Andrew Jackson, major general of the Tennessee militia, called out thousands of troops to crush the uprising. The big battle came at the Horseshoe Bend of the Tallapoosa River in March 1814. Jackson killed almost nine hundred warriors and took five hundred of their women and children prisoner. This shattered Red Stick resistance.

Jackson forced the Creeks into a treaty which handed over twenty million acres—two thirds of all their lands—to the Americans. This outcome delighted the land-hungry whites and made Jackson a hero to them. A thousand Creek warriors, refusing to accept the treaty, fled into north Florida with their families and black followers.

When the War of 1812 ended, the British left a fort on the eastern side of the Apalachicola River in Florida. It was about sixty miles below the United States border. The fort was heavily stocked with weapons and ammunition, including several cannon. Free blacks, descended from runaway slaves, had been living in this region for generations. They promptly made the fort their headquarters. Their farms and grazing lands stretched fifty miles up and down the river. Over three hundred blacks, including women and children, garrisoned the earthen fort, while perhaps another thousand lived in the surrounding region. The Negro Fort, as it was called, drew to the safety of its walls restless slaves from the plantations of Georgia and Alabama. The slaveholders along the border complained bitterly when they saw their human property drained away. They found a sympathetic ear in the army men stationed along the southern frontier, many of whose officers were themselves slaveholders. General Edmund Gaines, their commander at Fort Scott, wrote often to the Secretary of War in Washington about the menace of the Negro Fort, referring to the blacks as "outlaws," "pirates," and "murderers."

The blacks around the fort knew nothing of this. Their minds were on their families and farms, and the peace and liberty they were enjoying.

But among the slaveowners and their military friends plans were being forged to destroy that peace. What could they do, however, when the Negro Fort was deep inside Spanish territory? Some excuse was needed to violate the Spanish border and wipe out the black stronghold.

Not for Andrew Jackson, however. Now United

States army chief for the southern district, he wrote General Gaines in May 1816:

> I have little doubt of the fact, that this fort has been established by some villains for the purpose of rapine and plunder, and that it ought to be blown up, regardless of the ground on which it stands; and if your mind shall have formed the same conclusion, destroy it and return the stolen negroes and property to their rightful owners.

Remarkable that Jackson could so easily accuse the blacks of plotting rapine and plunder from a point sixty miles south of the United States. The truth was, the blacks were refugees, happy to stay away from the Americans. As for "stolen negroes," they had stolen only themselves in running away to freedom. They were no more "murderers" and "outlaws" than the patriots of 1776.

What rule of international law permitted General Jackson to order that a fort in foreign territory be blown up and its people, now free citizens of Spain, be turned into slaves?

No rule, only the desire of the slaveholders to enslave or destroy blacks who were enjoying their lives in peace and prosperity. And Jackson's knowledge that the Spanish were too weak to protect their citizens.

On General Gaines's order, United States supply vessels went down the river escorted by navy gunboats. Colonel Duncan L. Clinch commanded the regular troops, with five hundred Lower Creek Indians in support. The reason why the Creeks helped the Americans went back twenty years and more to the time when some Creek chiefs had entered into the treaties of New York and Colerain. They had bound themselves to surrender all runaway slaves among them and made themselves responsible for blacks held by the Florida Indians. Although once Creek in part, the Seminole now were separate and independent. They said those treaties were nonsense—the Creeks had no right to speak for them. Having failed to deliver on their treaty pledge, these Creeks were now allied with the whites in the first slave-catching expedition of the federal government.

In July 1816, navy gunboats headed up the river toward the Negro Fort. The idea, obviously, was to provoke fire from the fort that would provide the excuse for its destruction. From inside the fort came word that the blacks would fire on any ships that tried to pass them. If they could not hold the fort, they meant to blow it up. When the Americans called on them to surrender, the blacks opened fire. Ship batteries on the river answered. A hot shell whistled over earthworks and slammed into the fort's central powder magazine. Hundreds of barrels of gunpowder exploded, blowing the fort to pieces. When the Americans landed, they found 270 burned and mangled bodies, and took 64 prisoners, only a few of them uninjured. About thirty Seminole, who had intermarried with the blacks, died in the fort. Two of the survivors, a black and an Indian, symbols of the allied resistance, were handed over to the Creeks for execution.

The survivors able to travel were taken to Georgia and given to men who claimed to be the descendants of planters who generations before had owned the ancestors of these prisoners. No proof of identity was asked for; the prisoners were simply delivered upon claim. Some of the $200,000 worth of property captured in the fort was given to the Creeks who had accompanied the Americans, as their "share in the plunder."

The Spanish government protested this invasion and asked for the return of the property captured. But the Americans replied that it had belonged to the blacks, from whom it was taken in conquest, and not to the Spanish crown.

Twenty-two years later Congress paid a bonus to the officers and crews of the gunboats who had taken part in this massacre and piracy.

Nobody protested.

6

Andrew Jackson, Indian Fighter

The disaster at the Negro Fort broke black power on the Apalachicola. The settlers along the river fled east, leaving their homes, farms, and herds of cattle and horses for anyone to grab. They found shelter on the Suwannee, in the villages built up by Seminole Chief Bowlegs and his people. It took months for the shock to wear off. Meanwhile, they started homes once more, spreading down the seacoast as far as Tampa Bay.

Runaways continued to filter into Florida, to join black settlements scattered across the peninsula almost to St. Augustine. Besides the Suwannee, the larger communities were on the islands of the Great Wahoo Swamp, along the Withlacoochee River, in the Big Cypress Swamp, and on the St. Johns River.

Unable to forget their murdered families and friends, the blacks and the Seminole were determined to take revenge upon the Americans. They gathered crops, set by provisions, and obtained arms and ammunition from

British and Spanish traders, readying themselves for war. Early in 1817 General Gaines was reporting to Washington that hundreds of blacks were collecting at Suwannee and drilling in the use of arms.

Near Gaines's headquarters at Fort Scott was the Seminole village of Fowltown. Its chief warned Gaines to keep his soldiers away. Indignant at this challenge, Gaines, on November 21, 1817, sent a force that drove the Indians into the swamps, killed and wounded many, looted the village, and then burned it down.

The First Seminole War had begun.

Nine days later, the Seminole struck back by ambushing a party of soldiers under Lieutenant R. W. Scott, coming up the Apalachicola in a big open boat loaded with supplies for Fort Scott. The Indians killed all but six of the soldiers, as well as seven of their wives.

The press in the United States blazoned the news of the massacre. Editors denounced it as a savage sacrifice of human life. Americans were whipped into a rage against the Seminole for what was called an "unprovoked" attack.

"Unprovoked." It was the same accusing word used by President James Monroe in his message to Congress concerning the previous year's troubles with the Seminole. "The hostilities of this Tribe were unprovoked," he said. No mention was made of the massacre of blacks and Seminole at the Negro Fort. That moral outrage had vanished from the President's mind.

The facts about the origins of the First Seminole War were not given to the public. The war began without the American people having a word to say about it. They were never consulted, nor were their representatives in Congress. For two years General Gaines and the Secretary of War had exchanged messages about the Negro Fort, but no word about plans to invade foreign territory, destroy the fort, and enslave the blacks had been disclosed to Congress and the public.

Monroe, the new President, who had taken office in March 1817, appointed John C. Calhoun of South Carolina his Secretary of War. For the rest of his long public life, Calhoun would be distinguished for his ardent defense of slavery. Now he gave his energies to prosecuting the war against the Seminole.

A new Congress met in December. The Seminole question was taken up, but no one spoke of anything but the massacre of Lieutenant Scott's party and of Indian killings on the Georgia frontier. Slavery—a delicate issue the South was determined to keep Congress from discussing—was not mentioned. Thus, such major causes of the war as the drive for land and slaves and the massacre at the Negro Fort were never touched upon. It was easy, then, for the Administration to get from Congress the funds the President needed to fight the war.

To General Gaines went these instructions from Secretary of War Calhoun: "Should the Indians still refuse to make reparations for their outrages . . . it is the wish of the President that you consider yourself at liberty to march across the Florida line and to attack them. . . ."

Restless for action, General Jackson wrote to President Monroe: "Let it be signified to me through any channel that the possession of the Floridas would be desirable to the United States and in sixty days it will be accomplished."

Jackson got his orders to take command and bring the Seminole under control. In March 1818 he arrived at Fort Scott and started his campaign with a force of thirty-five hundred men. About two thousand were Creek warriors, fighting against their kinsmen; five hundred of the whites were regulars, and the rest mostly militia from Tennessee. With his greatly superior numbers, Jackson was able to destroy the Mikasuki towns. The Seminole were short of modern weapons and had to fight with bow and arrow. At Bowlegs's town, a few hundred blacks, fighting in their own companies and under their own officers, stayed west of the Suwannee and delayed Jackson's advance until the women and children could escape. Jackson found the village empty and destroyed it.

Now Jackson demanded the surrender of the Spanish fort at St. Mark's. The Indians and the blacks had been using it—with or without the commandant's permission—as an arsenal and headquarters. In his message to the Spanish commander, Jackson gave this justification of America's invasion of a foreign nation's soil:

> To chastise a savage foe, who, combined with a lawless band of Negro brigands, have for some time past been carrying on a cruel and unprovoked war against the citizens of the United States, has compelled the President to direct me to march my army into Florida.

So everyone but the United States was in the wrong.

When Jackson took the Spanish fort, he picked up the Scottish trader, Alexander Arbuthnot, long known for his friendly relations with the Florida Indians. At the Suwannee, Jackson captured Robert Armbrister, a veteran of the British marines, who had helped train black warriors. Jackson ordered a court-martial for these men, whom he labeled "foreign agents." They were both declared guilty of stirring up the Creeks to war against the United States, and sentenced to death. The court reconsidered Armbrister's case and reduced his sentence to fifty lashes and a year at hard labor. Jackson did not like this change of heart and ordered both prisoners executed. Two captured Indian leaders —lured aboard an American ship by the display of a British flag—were also put to death on his order. One was Chief Francis, a Creek prophet inspired by Tecumseh, and the other Himollemico, an old Red Stick chief. Without trial, without necessity, and almost without protest, Jackson had them executed.

On May 28, Jackson's troops took Pensacola. After only a few months, Spanish Florida was in American hands. General Jackson was more than ever the idol of the army and the white settlers of the South. Without a declaration of war upon Spain, an American general had captured Spanish forts and ousted their commandants, destroyed the villages of Indian and black citizens of Spain, and executed British subjects.

A conquest made so fast was almost too hard for the Monroe Administration to digest. The President's Cabinet and Congress debated whether to censure Jackson for violating the Constitution and assuming the power to make war. Some condemned him, but most praised him. Only a few had anything to say about the reason the war was begun.

One of those who commented was Congressman Charles Storrs of Connecticut. Speaking to the House, he said:

> We profess to be the only free government on earth—that our intercourse with foreign nations is characterized by moderation and justice—that our institutions are pure and unspotted—that our national character is beyond reproach. Above all, we profess to be Christians. Go—follow the track of this Christian army through the Floridas. It can easily be traced. Every footstep is trodden in blood. The path is strewed with the unbleached bones and livid carcasses of its slaughtered inhabitants. Survey this frightful waste of human life—the awful calamities which have been inflicted on our own species, and say if our posterity will not blush for their ancestors. . . .

The chief concern in Washington was that Jackson's invasion would upset the delicate maneuvers of diplomats negotiating with Spain to acquire Florida. There was no official censure of Jackson. Having approved the end he achieved, the people were not inclined to worry about the means.

Hardly a year after the invasion, Spain signed a treaty ceding Florida to the United States for the sum of five million dollars.

For the white land-grabbers and slaveholders it was a day of jubilation.

For the Seminole and the blacks, it was a day of mourning.

The Spanish explorer Juan Ponce de León, who claimed Florida for Spain in 1513. He died of an arrow wound inflicted by Indians, whom the invaders soon exterminated. The Seminole came later to Florida. THE NEW YORK PUBLIC LIBRARY PICTURE COLLECTION

Hernando de Soto, who led a large Spanish expedition to Florida and nearby regions in 1539. He observed the Creek culture from which Seminole life developed. THE NEW YORK PUBLIC LIBRARY PICTURE COLLECTION

The first artist to depict Indian life in what is now the United States was Jacques le Moyne de Morgues, mapmaker for the French Huguenots who established a colony on the St. Johns River in Florida in 1564. The French settlement was wiped out by the Spanish a year later. This is a view of the Florida shore, as engraved by Théodore de Bry after le Moyne's painting. RARE BOOK DIVISION, THE NEW YORK PUBLIC LIBRARY, ASTOR, LENOX AND TILDEN FOUNDATIONS

Beginning with Columbus, the Europeans who came to the New World sought to build fortunes by exploiting the people and their land. Ponce de León is shown here using guns and hounds against the Indians who resisted enslavement. RARE BOOK DIVISION, THE NEW YORK PUBLIC LIBRARY, ASTOR, LENOX AND TILDEN FOUNDATIONS

During the war against the Florida Indians and blacks, this lithograph was published to show how a Seminole village looked. Note the variety of house styles—some without walls for the warm climate, some closed in, some raised on stilts above marshy ground. THE NEW YORK PUBLIC LIBRARY PICTURE COLLECTION

Portrait of Micco Chlucco, a Seminole leader the naturalist William Bartram met in his exploration of Florida in the 1770's. The Philadelphia scientist gave us a vivid description of Seminole life in his *Travels* (1791). RARE BOOK DIVISION, THE NEW YORK PUBLIC LIBRARY, ASTOR, LENOX AND TILDEN FOUNDATIONS

The Florida Indians hold a council while the French colonists look on. An engraving by Bry after le Moyne's painting made in 1564. RARE BOOK DIVISION, THE NEW YORK PUBLIC LIBRARY, ASTOR, LENOX AND TILDEN FOUNDATIONS

Seminole village on the Apalachicola River in West Florida. From Comte Francis de Castelnau, *Vues et Souvenirs de l'Amérique du Nord,* published in 1842. AMERICAN HISTORY DIVISION, THE NEW YORK PUBLIC LIBRARY, ASTOR, LENOX AND TILDEN FOUNDATIONS

Andrew Jackson, painted by Asher B. Durand in the White House toward the end of the President's second term. Jackson won fame early for the ruthless way he crushed Indian resistance to white aggression. In 1818 he invaded Spanish Florida and destroyed many towns in which the Seminole and their black allies lived. COURTESY OF THE NEW YORK HISTORICAL SOCIETY, NEW YORK CITY

7

Land Grab

Jackson's invasion ripped apart the fabric of life for Indians and blacks in Florida. Their villages burned, their crops ruined, their families cut down, they wandered in search of new homes. The Red Sticks moved down to Tampa Bay. The Fowltown Indians left Georgia for the west bank of the Apalachicola. The Alachua dropped south about 120 miles, settling west of Lake Harris. The Mikasuki divided, some going west, others east and south. The blacks linked to these tribes moved with them, building their own villages next to the Indians'. Hundreds of the more recent runaway slaves, who had as yet formed no attachment to the Indians, made their way by boat to the Bahamas.

With the fighting over, the Seminole and the blacks tried to find the peace of prewar life. But those conditions would never return. The happy society William Bartram had seen was wrecked. One of the Seminole, Chief Sitarky, told how it felt: "When I walk about the woods now so desolate, and remember the numerous herds that once ranged through them, and the former prosperity of our nation, the tears come to my eyes." The Seminole had no say in the negotiations between Spain and the United States. Like cattle, they went with the land.

A clause in the treaty between Spain and the United States stated that everyone living in the ceded territories should be "admitted to the enjoyment of all privileges, rights and immunities of the citizens of the United States." The language would seem to mean that Indians and blacks as well as whites would become American citizens. But these were only words. Like the Indians and blacks long within American borders, the Indians and blacks of Florida would have no rights a white man was bound to respect.

As soon as Florida was taken over, slave-catchers began to raid at will into the Seminole lands. More pressure came from settlers who were cutting homes out of the wilderness. They forced the Seminole deeper and deeper into the peninsula. The whites did not hesitate to move onto Indian territory. They felt they had a superior right to it because, as Senator Thomas Benton put it, they "used it according to the intentions of the Creator." That tune was played by white Americans every time they got ready to take soil occupied by an "inferior" race. John Quincy Adams sounded it when he made this plea before the Supreme Court:

What is the Indian title? It is mere occupancy for the purpose of hunting. It is not like our tenures;

they have no idea of a title to the soil itself. It is overrun by them, rather than inhabited. It is not a true and legal possession.

The court agreed with him.

This was not a new excuse for grabbing someone else's land. Two hundred years earlier, the Puritans of Massachusetts said they "seized and settled" Indian lands "because they were not waving with fields of yellow corn duly fenced in with square-cut hawthorne."

The Holy Scriptures, said the Puritans, commanded the tilling of the earth: Increase and multiply, replenish the earth and subdue it [Gen. 1:28]. But the Indians did not believe that the Creator insisted that all his children be alike in their habits. A Pawnee chief said so when he talked to President Monroe in 1822:

The Great Spirit made us all—he made my skin red, and yours white; he placed us on this earth and intended that we should live differently from each other.

He made the whites to cultivate the earth, and feed on domestic animals; but he made us, red skins, to rove through the uncultivated woods and plains; to feed on wild animals and to dress with their skins. . . .

But the whites knew better what the Creator's intentions were. They stuck to the religious argument: it was the Almighty's command that the hunter give way to the farmer. They were sure they had a right to take away land from those who did not till it.

For those who would rather not lean so heavily on God's word, there was the doctrine of "natural law." Settlers who had come from overcrowded Europe had a right to take new land because they would cultivate it. The Indians should be pushed over to make room for these cultivators of the earth. One American, Hugh Brackenridge, went even further. In 1782 he recommended "extermination" for "the animals vulgarly called Indians." Because they had not made "a better use of the land," he said, they had no natural right to it.

By now, of course, the Americans had already taken territory far beyond their capacity to cultivate. And as they thrust into unneeded Indian lands, they were leaving behind vast forests of neglected land. To counter the few who pointed out such facts, John Quincy Adams had a defense. He said the population was growing so fast that if Indian barriers were not torn down they would deprive *future* generations of the land they would need. He assumed that Indians had no right to provide for *their* posterity.

Another kind of argument, phrased poetically, was mustered to dispossess the Indians. The whites would change the barren wilderness of the Indians into a beautiful civilization. Congressman George F. Strother described this vision in 1819 when he defended Jackson's invasion of Seminole country:

The Western frontier is that portion of the world where civilization is making the most rapid and ex-

> tensive conquest of the wilderness, carrying in its train the Christian religion and all the social virtues. It is the point where the race is most progressive; establish but the principle, that the God of nature has limited your march in that direction—that the Indian is lord paramount of that wide domain, around which justice and religion have drawn a circle which you dare not pass—the progress of mankind is arrested and you condemn one of the most beautiful and fertile tracts of the earth to perpetual sterility as the hunting ground of a few savages.

The Spanish treaty of 1819 handed the Americans not only Florida but all Spanish territory as far west as the Rockies. It was a huge piece of continent that would require generations to develop. But if the Florida Indians thought this would give the whites more than enough to occupy them, they were wrong, for it was just at this time that the first organized movement to oust all Indians from the country east of the Mississippi sprang up.

It was not Western pioneers who fathered it, but Easterners. Nor was it a movement born out of need for land. Georgians boasted publicly that their state had all the cheap land anyone could want.

No, the drive for removal of the Indians had these reasons behind it:

The whites wanted all the land they could get.

The Southern states wanted to rid themselves of the legal problems arising from Indians living within their jurisdiction.

Some people in both North and South thought the Indians would be better off if they could live away from the evil influences of white civilization.

The strongest force for removal of the Indians would, of course, be Andrew Jackson. While the Seminole waited anxiously to find out the government's intentions, their old enemy was made governor of the territory. Jackson spent only three months on the job in Florida. Micanopy, the head chief of the Alachua bands, hoped to negotiate a treaty, but the governor would have none of it. To him the Indians were subjects of the United States, not a sovereign people. He thought it nonsense to make treaties with them as though they were an independent people.

Meanwhile, in Washington, the government debated what to do about the Seminole. Secretary Calhoun proposed two possibilities: to concentrate all the Seminole in one place in Florida, or to remove them from the peninsula altogether.

Get rid of the Indians! That was what the white settlers urged. The easiest thing to do, they thought, was to send them north to rejoin the Creeks in Georgia and Alabama. That was Jackson's own choice at first. He said so to a congressional committee on September 2, 1822, and added: "This must be done, or the frontier will be much weakened by the Indian settlements, and be a perpetual harbor for our slaves. These runaway slaves . . . must be removed from the Floridas, or scenes of murder and confusion will result."

The opinion of so popular a general had great weight. He stuck to his removal policy when he became President, and so did most of the Presidents who came after him.

When Jackson left Florida, William DuVal replaced him. The new governor found the Indians weak and hungry, but their spirit unbroken. They were so uncertain of the future that they would not put in crops, lest the whites take their fields. Like Jackson, DuVal urged Washington to send the Seminole back to the Creeks. The Seminole made it clear they would not consent to this. Neither would the whites of Georgia. Then ship them west of the Mississippi, said DuVal. The government had already done this with other Eastern Indians. It was the first time anyone had suggested it for the Seminole.

Finally, the Monroe Administration made up its mind. The Seminole would be obliged to move to a reservation. Call the Indians together, Calhoun ordered, and tell them this is what the United States insists upon. At this time there were thirty-five principal Indian bands in Florida, numbering about four thousand men, women, and children. Living among them were eight hundred blacks.

A council of Seminole consisting of some thirty Indian bands, assembled at Moultrie Creek in the fall of 1823. They came reluctantly, in the faint hope that a settlement with the whites would forever after leave them in peace. They chose Neamathla, a head chief, as their spokesman. James Gadsden of South Carolina led the United States negotiators. He was blunt: take the territory we assign you, or what General Jackson did to you twice, we will do again.

It ended with the Indians signing a treaty pretty much as the whites dictated it. The Seminole gave up all claim to Florida except for a reservation of four million acres north of Charlotte's River. Thus they handed over to the United States twenty-eight million acres. In return, the Seminole got a guarantee of peaceable possession of their reservation, including "protection against all persons whatsoever" and a ban on "all white persons from hunting, settling, or otherwise intruding upon said lands."

Other clauses provided some equipment and livestock and cash annuities for twenty years, funds for a school, an agent, interpreter, blacksmith, and gunsmith. The cash value of all these amounted to $221,000. Translated into payment per acre, it meant the United States got twenty-eight million acres for about three fourths of a cent per acre.

A major concession made to the white slaveholders was the promise of the Seminole to try to prevent runaway slaves from concentrating in their territory.

Nothing was said in the treaty about how long it was to last. Later the whites would interpret that to mean that there was no guarantee the Seminole could stay on the reservation for any definite period. The Seminole would claim the duration of the treaty was certainly twenty years, because that was the period annuities were pledged for.

Why did the Indians sign at Moultrie Creek? Gadsden explained to Calhoun in a letter:

> It is not necessary to disguise the fact to you that the treaty effected was in a degree a treaty of imposition. The Indians would never have voluntarily assented to the terms had they not believed that we had both the power and disposition to compel obedience.

Pleased with the result, Calhoun told the President he should assure the Seminole they now had "a permanent home for themselves and their posterity."

Gadsden did not see it in quite that way. He wrote his friend Andrew Jackson that the idea behind the treaty was to get the Seminole clustered together so they could one day be moved west more easily.

"Whatever the moral judgement passed on it," wrote the historian John K. Mahon, "no one can deny that this treaty was the first in a series of disasters to befall the Indians of Florida."

8

If You Don't Like It, Move!

Again the Seminole had to move. By the terms of the treaty, they were to give up their farms, their livestock, their villages, and start over again on the reservation. Their chiefs had agreed to it, but most of the Seminole did not want to move. Whether the whites intended it or not, the new land turned out to be bad. Governor DuVal himself rode over it and said it was "by far the poorest and most miserable region I ever beheld."

The Seminole suffered terribly from hunger in the first years of transition. The rations provided by treaty were too scanty to sustain life, and they were forced to live on roots. The new fields they had to open were parched by so bad a drought the first year that the crops were ruined. The agent to the Seminole, Colonel Gad Humphreys, had to plead with the government not to reduce their rations when someone proposed it as a means of speeding their move to the reservation.

Tormented by hunger, and uncertain of their northern boundary, which had not yet been surveyed, the

Seminole roamed through the country in search of food. White settlers had already squatted on public lands close by, and tensions mounted as the Indians preyed on the settlers' cattle. Some of the Seminole, finding the reservation intolerable, moved back across the Suwannee. The whites threatened them and tried to get the militia to drive them back into the reservation.

Typical was the behavior of one white settler reported by Colonel Humphreys: "He often, in a light manner, speaks of shooting them [the Seminole], and has been heard to say that he would dispatch one with as little scruple as he would a wolf."

The Florida legislature passed a law against roaming Indians. It permitted anyone to seize any Indian found outside the reservation and take him to a justice of the peace. If the Indian was without a pass from the agent, he was given thirty-nine stripes on his bare back and his gun was taken from him. The oppressive and humiliating law was no mischance. A legislator told Colonel Humphreys its true purpose:

> It is found impossible to bring them [the Seminole] to negotiate for a removal from the territory, and the only course, therefore, which remains for us to rid ourselves of them is to adopt such a mode of treatment towards them, as will induce them to acts that will justify their expulsion by force.

The pressure was increased daily by the demand whites made for blacks who they said were their runaway slaves. Many of the blacks had been born among the Seminole; others had been purchased by them. A common trick of the white man was to sell a black to an Indian and then claim him as a runaway. The Indian had paid, but he could not show legal papers because he received none from the white, having relied on the white's honesty. When slave-hunters demanded that he hand over the black, the Indian was determined not to. If the Indian went to law for a remedy, it was his word against a white's, and no one believed him.

Once the black was in a white man's hands, there wasn't the least prospect that he would ever be returned. The black man himself, whether slave or free, was treated like a mule: he was allowed to say nothing about his own right to liberty. His voice was silenced. Those who claimed to own him could always find another white to testify to their claim. It was useless for either red or black to enter into legal contest with a white slaveholder before a slaveholding white judge.

Slave-hunters brazenly raided for blacks inside the Seminole reservation. When the Indians protested against this violation of the treaty, the reply came—the Secretary of War has given them permission. Even Governor DuVal found this intolerable. What kind of "left-handed justice" is this, he asked the Secretary of War, "which gives all that is demanded to our citizens and which withholds justice from this cheated, abused, and persecuted race."

By 1826 the Seminole-white conflict was close to a crisis. Most of the Indians were now living within the reservation, but hunger still forced some of them to seek food outside. The Florida whites clamored for their removal to the West. To awe the Indians with a display of white power, the Administration invited some of the leading Seminole chiefs to Washington. Seven came, among them Neamathla and Tuchose Emathla, called John Hicks by the whites. With Abraham, a Seminole black, acting as interpreter, Hicks said his people would never go west. "Here our navel strings were first cut," he said, "and the blood from them sunk into the earth and made the country dear to us."

Nothing came of the meeting. Back in Florida, the whites grew more and more rapacious, the Indians more and more angry. When the killings on both sides mounted, Washington centralized Florida's military command under Colonel Duncan Clinch. He posted small units of troops to maintain order.

Under the pressure of the white danger, the Florida Indian bands moved toward unity. They chose John Hicks to be the first chief of the Seminole nation. Early in 1829, he complained that the whites were unrelenting in their demands. The Seminole had handed over many of the blacks "with no masters," yet the whites asked for more. Did they mean to go on until they had taken everything from the Seminole?

They did. Even as Hicks spoke, Washington had come to a final decision about the Southeastern Indians. John Quincy Adams, now President and nearing the end of his only term, decided that the Indians must be removed west of the Mississippi.

By this time the spearhead of Southern frontiersmen

had crossed the Mississippi and was penetrating Louisiana, Arkansas, and Missouri. Behind them, white settlers were still trying to take over enclaves of land the Indians clung to. In northeast Georgia, in western North Carolina, in southern Tennessee, in eastern Alabama, in northern Mississippi, and in Florida, some sixty-five thousand Indians lived in what they considered to be their own domains. These were the Five Civilized Tribes: Cherokees, Creeks, Choctaws, Chickasaws, and the Seminole.

Like the Seminole, the Southeastern tribes were farmers as well as hunters. For the last two or three generations they had given their labor to the soil. White traders, government agents, and missionaries had encouraged them to fence their farms, use the plow, and raise cotton and corn for the market. Hundreds of Protestant missionaries had worked among the Cherokees, Choctaws, and Chickasaws for almost twenty years, educating the children in the agricultural, mechanical, and household arts. They came bearing the blessings, as they saw them, of literacy and Christianity. The government encouraged the work by appropriating special funds.

By the mid-1820's many Indian leaders had built up valuable plantations, mills, and trading posts. The Cherokees and Choctaws especially were proud of the progress they had made in adapting themselves to the white man's civilization. But this did not lessen their love of their homeland. They wanted to enjoy their new way of life here on what was left of their ancient grounds.

But Adams, and now Andrew Jackson, the incoming President, asked that the Indians be cleared out of the path of civilization. The old argument that the farmer had a superior right to the land over the hunter sounded plausible to many so long as the tribes involved were "savage." But here was the Cherokee nation, which had embraced agriculture, devised its own alphabet, established schools and newspapers and churches. How could these people be removed, in all justice? Had not John Quincy Adams himself said that *cultivated* Indian lands would *always* be respected?

The damned Cherokees! They had turned to civilized ways for the perverse purpose of confounding the white men who wanted to get rid of them. The whole trouble with the Cherokees, Calhoun told a Cabinet meeting, was precisely their progress in civilization.

Washington sent agents to urge the Indians to move west, where there was ample wilderness for hunting. But why should we go, said the Cherokees: we are "unequivocably determined never again to pursue the chase as heretofore."

It was embarrassing. But men have always been able to find a reason to justify their desires. The whites came up with a new ground for expelling the Cherokees: they had no right to alter their condition and become farmers! The governor of Georgia, where many of the Cherokees lived, said that yes, God wanted Georgian soil to be tilled, but by the *white* man, not the Indians.

Just as the Cherokee were realizing the goal of white civilization that so many had advocated for them, the

American government was abandoning it and them.

Jackson entered the White House in 1829. In his first message to Congress he took up the Indian question:

> The people . . . of every state . . . submit to you the interesting question whether something cannot be done, consistently with the rights of the States, to preserve this much-injured race [Indians]. . . . I suggest, for your consideration, the propriety of setting apart an ample district west of the Mississippi, and without the limits of any State or Territory now formed, to be guaranteed to the Indian tribes as long as they shall occupy it. . . .
>
> There they may be secured in the enjoyment of governments of their own choice subject to no other control from the United States than such as may be necessary to preserve peace on the frontier and between the several tribes. . . . This emigration should be voluntary, for it would be as cruel as unjust to compel the aborigines to abandon the graves of their fathers and seek a home in a distant land. But they should be as distinctly informed that, if they remain within the limits of the States, they must be subject to their laws.

The Indians can no longer exist as independent nations within the states, Jackson was saying. They must either move west or become subject to the laws of the states.

Confident of the President's backing, four Southern

states moved against the Indians. They passed bills nullifying the legal force of Indian customs. Heavy penalties were levied against anyone who might enact or enforce tribal law. And punishment was threatened for those who would interfere with or discourage Indian emigration. The Georgians went furthest, providing for the use of force to get the Indians out.

The Indians protested.

Jackson was blunt: you have no hope of relief from the federal government, he said. If you don't like it, move.

The Cherokees took their plea for recognition as a self-governing people to the United States Supreme Court. They won their case. In *Worcester* v. *Georgia,* Chief Justice Marshall upheld them. Georgia had no right to extend its law over Cherokee territory. It was contrary to treaties and the Constitution.

But victory in the courts did not protect the Cherokees. President Jackson refused to honor the court's decision. "John Marshall has made his decision; now let him enforce it," the President said.

A fierce debate over the President's removal policy took place in Congress. Senator Theodore Frelinghuysen of New Jersey took the floor to argue that the Indians had a superior title to the land:

I proceed to a discussion of those principles which . . . sustain the claims of the Indians to all their political and civil rights as by them asserted. And

> here I insist that, by immemorial possession, as the original tenants of the soil, they hold a title beyond and superior to the British Crown and her colonies and to all adverse pretensions of our confederation and subsequent Union. . . . No argument can shake the political maxim that where the Indian has always been, he enjoys an absolute right still to be, in the free exercise of his own modes of thought, government, and conduct. . . .
>
> The confiding Indian listened to our professions of friendship; we called him brother, and he believed us. . . . We have crowded the tribes upon a few miserable acres on our Southern frontier: it is all that is left to them of their once boundless forests; and still, like the horse-leech, our insatiated cupidity cries, give! give!

A new concern for human rights was emerging, especially in New England and the East. Freedom for the black slave, reform of prisons, improvement of treatment for the mentally ill, temperance, public education, the rights of women, and now justice for the Indian were causes that began to draw passionate support. Petitions signed by thousands flooded into Congress to protest the removal bill. Speeches, editorials, and articles were reprinted in pamphlet form to muster popular support.

What about our treaties with the Indians, people asked. Didn't they recognize Indian sovereignty and Indian rights?

Georgia's Governor George G. Gilmer had a ready answer:

> Treaties were expedients by which ignorant, intractable, and savage people were induced without bloodshed to yield up what civilized people had a right to possess by virtue of that command of the Creator delivered to man upon his formation—be fruitful, multiply, and replenish the earth, and subdue it.

He was saying treaties were merely tricks to get without force what the civilized white man wanted from the savage Indian.

"Is it one of the prerogatives of the white man," asked Senator Frelinghuysen, "that he may disregard the dictates of moral principles, when an Indian shall be concerned?"

It seemed that it was.

Jackson had his way. The Indian Removal Act of 1830 was adopted by Congress in a close vote. On the surface, it looked humane. The government was permitted to enter into treaties trading land in the West for Indian lands in the East. A permanent guarantee of possession of the lands was given, as well as compensation for improvements already made, and aid for the emigrants. The act authorized removal *only* if the Indians gave consent. But anyone who knew Jackson's history, and the history of the frontier, understood that the use of force would be inevitable.

Congress put up only half a million dollars to compensate the Indians for the loss of lands and the expense of moving and getting settled west of the Mississippi.

Some Indians moved rapidly, ceding their lands in the East. The Choctaws were the first. Only a few months after the Removal Act was passed, Secretary of War John H. Eaton induced them to sign a treaty removing them from their old homes in Mississippi. "Through the use of hypocrisy, bribes, lies, suppression of critics, and intimidation," wrote historian Edward Pessen, Eaton secured approval of a treaty that was despised by most of the Indians.

In 1832 the Creeks signed, and then the Chickasaws. The Cherokees stubbornly refused to go. Year after year they resisted in every way they could, while white speculators and Southern politicians got more and more impatient. Finally a small group of Cherokees, without authority to act for their nation, entered into a fraudulent treaty with the government, agreeing to removal. The army moved in to enforce it. Fifteen thousand Cherokees—men, women, and children—trudged along throughout the winter months, hurried on their way by soldiers, so that they could not even stop to take care of the sick or bury their dead. Four thousand—a fourth of the Cherokee nation—died on this Trail of Tears, a forced migration that one historian has said "approached the horrors created by the Nazi handling of subjected peoples."

What about the Seminole?

9

Osceola, the Young Militant

One after another the Civilized Tribes were lined up for removal west. From across their borders, the Florida whites watched the Choctaws go, then the Creeks, then the Chickasaws. But the Seminole stayed where they were. Had Andrew Jackson forgotten them?

Petitions barraged the President to remind him to get the Seminole out of Florida. The Indians were still suffering on their reservation. How badly is revealed in a petition the Florida legislative council sent Congress, begging it to oust the Indians. For once, the whites found it expedient to tell the truth:

> The Treaty of 1823 deprived them [the Seminole] of their cultivated fields and of a region fruitful of game, and has placed them in a wilderness where the earth yields no corn, and where even the precarious advantages of the chase are in a great measure denied them. . . .
>
> They are thus left the wretched alternative of

starving within their limits, or roaming among the whites, to prey upon their cattle. Many in the Nation, it seems, annually die of starvation; but as might be expected, the much greater proportion of those who are threatened with want, leave their boundaries in pursuit of the means of subsistence, and between these and the white settlers is kept up an unceasing contest.

Not the plight of the Seminole, but the anger of the whites, impelled Jackson to act. In 1832 he sent James Gadsden to Florida to negotiate a removal treaty. (It was Gadsden who nine years earlier had put through the Moultrie Creek Treaty.) Gadsden met with several Seminole chiefs at Payne's Landing in May. The government will not go on feeding you year after year, he told the Seminole. Your situation will only get worse if you refuse to move. The meeting ended in a treaty that called for seven Seminole chiefs to visit the Indian Territory west of the Mississippi to study its suitability as a new home. If "they" were satisfied, then the Seminole would move.

The treaty spelled out what would happen *if* the all-important condition was met: that is, *if* the Western land should prove satisfactory. The Seminole would then voluntarily leave Florida within three years, one third going each year. They would give up all claims to their Florida land in return for grants amounting to about $80,000. (That amount came to two cents for each of the four million acres on the reservation.) Finally, the Seminole would rejoin the Creek nation, taking up land assigned the Creeks in the West and sharing in the annual payments Congress set aside for the Creeks.

How could the Seminole accept such conditions? They would be giving up not only their homeland but their independence as a nation. What would happen to the blacks with whom they had established so many close ties? And who was the "they" who had to be satisfied—the delegation of seven, or the nation as a whole?

The marks of fifteen chiefs and subchiefs are on the paper, but Micanopy, for one, denied he had ever touched the pen. Thomas McKenney, for years Superintendent of Indian Affairs, called the treaty an open fraud, "a foul blot upon the escutcheon of the nation." It is likely that it was signed in the face of the threat of overwhelming force—which Gadsden had not hesitated to apply in 1823—made against a people now even weaker than before.

Now came the testing of that "if." In October 1832, seven Seminole chiefs with their black interpreter Abraham, and the government agent, John Phagan, crossed the Mississippi to examine the Indian Territory.

Not even waiting for them to return, President Jackson sent commissioners west to get from the delegation—while they were isolated from their people—a statement that the country was suitable and the Creeks were willing to unite with the Seminole. The commission intended for the treaty to be signed before the Seminole could return to Florida and report to their nation, giving it a chance to determine what to do.

Jackson got what he wanted—once more. His agents obtained a treaty at Fort Gibson in March 1833. The Seminole delegation signed it without any authority from their people.

There are two crucial points in this document. The delegation states they are satisfied with the land allotted to their people; and it is agreed that the Seminole "shall commence the removal to their new home as soon as the Government will make arrangements for their emigration satisfactory to the Seminole nation."

At the bottom of the treaty appear the marks of the chiefs and the signatures of the commissioners and some witnesses. Three of the chiefs later denied that they had signed the treaty. Army officers claimed that Phagan had wheedled and bullied the chiefs into signing. There is evidence of trickery by the whites in the way a vital point is phrased. The Payne's Landing Treaty had said, "Should *they* be satisfied." The passage as reworded at Fort Gibson said, "Should *this delegation* be satisfied."

Professor Mahon, after studying the record, wrote:

> I believe that Agent John Phagan prepared the treaty, forced it upon the Indians, and then secured the acquiescence of the commissioners without their bothering to inquire into it. Part of his game

was the stipulation in the document that he himself should be agent for the Seminole removal. This the Indians swallowed with the rest. He had also, when quoting from the Treaty of Payne's Landing, altered the words.

When the Seminole exploring party returned to Florida in April, they wanted to call the nation together to hear their report. Agent Phagan refused to allow it. There's no point, he said; the question of removal has been settled. All that remained was for the government to order the terms of the treaty carried out. This it could not do until the Senate had ratified the related treaties of Payne's Landing and Fort Gibson. Not for another year would it get around to it.

Meanwhile, Phagan was removed as agent, and the tall, powerful Georgian, Wiley Thompson, put in his place. After serving with Jackson in the Creek War, Thompson had become a general in the state militia. For six terms in Congress he had been a supporter of Jackson's Indian-removal policy. Now Jackson gave him the job of getting the Seminole out of Florida.

First he tried talking it over with the Indians. Neither the land nor the climate nor the prospects of subsistence in the Indian Territory were any good, the Indians said. Why should they leave the familiar forests and the fields they had cleared and tilled for the strange prairies and severe climate of the West? Next to the lands offered them lived other tribes which might prove hostile. And what need was there for them to put themselves under the control of the more powerful Creeks, from whom they had seceded almost a century before?

They were greatly concerned over what might happen to the blacks who lived among them—many of them wives or husbands of the Indians, or their children. The Creeks were sure to renew claims upon some of them. Others were recent runaways from the whites. If the Indians were assembled for removal, white slaveholders would rush in to demand their property. Even blacks who had been legally purchased would not be safe, as the Seminole had bitter reason to know. Nor would free blacks, no matter how long they had been their own masters.

No, the Indians told Thompson, we won't move. We were given twenty years under the Treaty of Moultrie Creek. We still have nine years to stay in Florida.

They meant what they said. Thompson soon had proof of it.

Reports came that the Seminole were buying unusually large amounts of powder and lead. Alarmed, Thompson called the chiefs together in October 1834. We're not here to talk about whether you go or stay, he said, but about *how* removal is to be carried out.

That night the Seminole met in their own council. (There were spies to let the agent know what was said.) Some of the chiefs felt the bands had no choice but to migrate; the whites were too strong to be resisted. Micanopy, the principal chief, was opposed. By his side, giving him ardent support, was a Seminole warrior named Osceola. The young warriors will never consent to move, he said.

This was the first time the rising influence of the new Seminole leader was to affect the whites. Now about thirty-five, Osceola had come from Creek country in Alabama. After the crushing defeat by Jackson in the Creek War, he and his mother had migrated to Florida with the Red Sticks. His name came from the Creek words, Asi-yahola, meaning the "black-drink singer." He was not a chief by inheritance, but his boldness and brilliance made him a natural leader.

Osceola's militant stand was adopted. The chiefs went back into the sessions with Thompson, united for resistance. We will not leave, they told him. The agent was furious, but careful. Give them time, he advised Washington, and they may change their minds.

That winter, one of Florida's worst cold waves struck. The bitter weather killed the Seminole's cattle and cut off food supplies. The suffering of the Indians only stiffened their resistance.

As General Clinch built up his military strength, Thompson tried talks once more. The chiefs were willing to come, for they hoped to get food for their hungry people.

To an assembly of 150 headmen and warriors, Thompson read this letter from the Great White Father himself:

My Children—I am sorry to have heard that you have been listening to bad counsel. You know me, and you know that I would not deceive, nor advise you to do anything that was unjust or injurious. Open your ears and attend to what I shall now say to you. They are the words of a friend, and the words of truth.

The white people are settling around you. The game has disappeared from your country. Your people are poor and hungry. All this you have perceived for some time. . . .

My Children, I have never deceived nor will I ever deceive any of the red people. Even if you had a right to stay, how could you live where you now are? You have sold all your country. You have not a piece as large as a blanket to sit down upon. What is to support yourselves, your women, and children. The tract you have ceded will soon be surveyed and sold, and immediately afterwards will be occupied by a white population. You will soon be in a state of starvation. You will commit depredations upon the property of our citizens. You will be resisted, punished, perhaps killed.

Now is it not better peaceably to remove to a fine, fertile country, occupied by your own kindred, and where you can raise all the necessaries of life, and where game is yet abundant? The annuities payable to you, and the other stipulations made in your favor, will make your situation comfortable, and will enable you to increase and improve. If, therefore, you had a right to stay where you now are, still every true friend would advise you to remove. But you have no right to stay, and you must go. I am very desirous that you should go peaceably and voluntarily. You shall be comfortably taken care of, and kindly treated on the road, and when you arrive in your new country, provisions will be issued to you for a year, so that you can have ample time to provide for your future support.

But lest some of your rash young men should forcibly oppose your arrangements for removal, I have ordered a large military force to be sent among you. I have directed the commanding officer, and likewise the agent, your friend, General Thompson, that every reasonable indulgence be held out to you. But I have also directed that one third of your people, as provided for in the treaty, be removed during the present season. If you listen to the voice of friendship and truth, you will go quietly and voluntarily. But should you listen to the bad birds that are always flying about you, and refuse to move, I have then directed the commanding officer to remove you by force. This will be done. I pray the Great Spirit, therefore, to incline you to do what is right.

Your Friend,
A. Jackson

Washington, February 16, 1835

This time Thompson succeeded in getting sixteen chiefs to sign a paper accepting the Treaty of Payne's Landing. Four chiefs refused. In a rage, Thompson went beyond his authority and struck their names from the list of chiefs recognized by the United States. He added Micanopy's too: he was absent on a plea of illness.

There is a legend that Osceola walked up to the table as though to sign the treaty. Instead of taking the pen, he drew out his hunting knife and plunged it into the treaty paper, pinning it to the table. "This," he said, "is the only treaty I make with the whites."

Six weeks later Thompson arrested Osceola and put him in irons. The Seminole was wild with rage. Being chained was an insult he could never forgive. Powerless in prison, he decided to use deception to get out. He signed the document certifying the Treaty of Payne's Landing. But Thompson demanded even more in exchange for Osceola's freedom. The Seminole then agreed to use his influence to promote removal. Runners went out, while Osceola stayed in prison, and brought in seventy-nine Seminole willing to go west. Then Thompson let Osceola go. At once, the Indian began to organize his people to defend their right to their homeland.

10

Black Resistance

The whites of Florida felt there was little to worry about. The Seminole were a peaceful people—even cowardly, some said contemptuously. Let them try to resist removal and they would be put down in a few weeks. General Clinch knew better. "If a sufficient military force is not sent," he warned Washington, "the whole frontier may be laid waste by a combination of the Indians, Indian Negroes, and the Negroes on the plantations."

That was just what the whites had overlooked—the grimly tenacious power this combination of forces would be welded into by the passion to be free.

Secret preparations for resistance had long been under way. One of its key leaders was the very man the whites believed to be doing everything possible to encourage Seminole removal—Abraham, the black interpreter.

Who was Abraham? We would like to know much more about him than the records tell us, as we would about all the red and black leaders of the Seminole resistance. The trouble is, history is usually written from the point of view of the conqueror. And when you have a "civilized" nation fighting a "savage" foe, the record of what happened is largely in the hands of government officials and reporters who see people and events through blinded eyes.

Race prejudice was the ruling passion of the age. The enemy forces fighting the United States consisted of two peoples—Indians and blacks—both despised by whites. Yet they displayed a courage and skill that commanded respect. The army and the press found themselves in a dilemma. They wanted to be accurate—for the army, especially, it was vital to know the facts concerning the enemy. But many of its officers were Southerners. If they let themselves see the blacks as human beings fighting for their families and for freedom, they would be arousing sympathy for the black cause and helping the abolition movement. Neither could journalists bring themselves to present a picture of the enemy that would clash with old prejudices or arouse public sympathy.

So what we know about men like Abraham has to be pieced together from many scattered sources. Most often the blacks are seen as an undefined dark power, a threat to the security of slavery. The scanty evidence left us is contradictory, and the historian has to judge what is more likely the truth and what is distortion or a lie.

Abraham was born around 1790. In his youth he was a slave to a doctor in Pensacola, probably trained to be his domestic servant. Later, whites always mention his courtly manners. He was tall and slim, and had a squint in his right eye. He was probably one of the Pensacola slaves offered freedom by the British when they recruited blacks to strengthen their forces against the United States in the War of 1812. Abraham showed up later at one of the Seminole towns on the Suwannee, where he came under the protection of Chief Micanopy. Abraham's knowledge of both English and the Muskogee tongue of the Seminole led to his being used as an interpreter, and his familiarity with white life led the Seminole to accept him as a counselor as well. He lived in a black village occupied chiefly by runaway slaves from Georgia, who looked to him for leadership. His first step into prominence came when Micanopy chose him to accompany the Seminole delegation to Washington in 1826. On his return, he was liberated for his "many and faithful services and great merits."

He married the widow of Bowlegs, one of the Seminole chiefs. They had several children. In 1832, Abraham was one of the two black interpreters at the Treaty of Payne's Landing, and the next year he went with the delegation that inspected the Indian Territory. By now, according to white observers, he seems to have been the chief counselor, or "sense-bearer," to Micanopy. He has "as much influence in the nation as any man," wrote

John Lee Williams, who thought him sensible, shrewd, ambitious, and very intelligent. Major Thomas Childs wrote that Abraham's influence is "unlimited."

The whites were anxious to win that influence on behalf of removal, and it is apparent that Abraham pretended to fall in with them. In reality, however, he was determined to encourage the Indians to resist removal, which he knew would be fatal to the blacks. In public he functioned as interpreter at the many meetings between the Seminole and the government agent. Behind the scenes, he strengthened the head chief's will to resist.

Abraham realized that the Seminole could find valuable allies among the slaves on the sugar plantations along the St. Johns River. Those blacks knew well how much better life among the Seminole would be than slavery among the whites, for several of the Seminole blacks had relatives on the plantations. The slaves listened eagerly to the promises of freedom Abraham and other emissaries offered when they made secret visits to the plantations. As soon as war breaks out, Abraham told them, be ready to rise in revolt. Your interests and ours are the same.

Nor did Abraham neglect the free blacks of East Florida. About two hundred of them lived around St. Augustine. They had more to lose by aiding the Seminole resistance than did the slaves, but they had ample reason to help. United States law and custom deprived them of the privileges they had enjoyed under Spanish rule, and now the territory had clamped a harsh black code upon them. So they were eager to supply information, together with food and ammunition.

Working with Abraham to win allies among the slaves and the blacks was a fierce old black man, John Caesar. He had either been born among the Seminole or had lived with them so long he was thoroughly identified as an "Indian Negro." He was a dependent of King Philip of the St. Johns Indians and performed the same services for him as Abraham did for Micanopy.

A sudden restlessness among the plantation slaves came to the attention of their masters. In October, General Clinch reported that "some of the most respectable planters fear that there is already a secret and improper communication carried on between the refractory Indians, Indian Negroes, and some of the plantation Negroes." Clinch announced the Seminole must assemble at Tampa Bay for migration by the first of next year or they would be deported by force.

Some of the Seminole chiefs became convinced that resistance was hopeless. They decided they would do as the whites wanted, and move west. Among them was Charley Emathla, a chief with great influence. Militants strongly opposed to removal decided he must be made an example. Since he was about to leave Florida, Emathla had sold his cattle to the whites, taking payment in gold. He was on his way home with a small group of his people when he was surrounded by a larger band led by Osceola. A bitter argument over removal took place. It ended when Osceola shot Emathla dead. The gold was found in a pouch on the dead man's body, but Osceola said no man should take it: it was the price of the red man's blood. He flung the coins into the forest and left the chief's carcass for the wolves and vultures.

The news brought panic to the whites and to those Indian headmen who like Charley Emathla were prepared to yield. Five chiefs with five hundred of their people fled to Fort Brooke, seeking army protection against Osceola's war party.

The governor recruited five hundred mounted horsemen as a militia force and moved them from one place to another to prevent the attacks that were rumored to be imminent. When a military baggage train became separated from the main party, Osceola's band ambushed and captured it. A week later, at Christmas time, warriors led by King Philip and John Caesar raided the valuable sugar plantations along the St. Johns and one after another plundered and burned them, aided by rebellious slaves. That the plantation slaves were joining the Indians was, as one white officer said, "the very worst feature of the whole of this war." Whites who had clamored for war in the hope of seizing and enslaving the Seminole blacks now saw their own plantations destroyed and four hundred of their own slaves liberated. The whites fled in terror. Hysteria seized Florida and spread into adjacent states when the news came of a slave uprising on the St. Johns.

In Washington, President Jackson was both amazed and enraged. Never patient with the Indians, he ordered General Clinch to "inflict just punishment for outrages so unpunished."

The Seminole were acting on a plan they had drawn up many months before. As soon as the plantations had been destroyed, the Indians, anticipating retaliation by the whites, had disappeared. In hiding, they watched for their next chance to strike. A major goal was to eliminate Wiley Thompson. Late in December, the moment came. Only one military company was on duty at Fort King, Thompson's headquarters, while two others were marching from Fort Brooke along a hundred-mile road to strengthen Fort King.

Burning for revenge against Thompson, Osceola waited in ambush around Fort King on the afternoon of December 28. He watched Thompson and his dinner companion, a Lieutenant Smith, go for a walk in the woods outside the palisade. At a signal, the Indians fired upon them. Both men fell, Thompson with fourteen wounds and Smith with two. The Indians took their scalps and then caught the sutler and his two clerks at dinner. Firing through the windows, they killed the three men. The officer in command of the fort heard the shooting and thought it was Indians trying to lure the whites out. He didn't know Thompson had gone outside. He closed the gates and waited inside with his company. When he realized what had happened, the Indians had vanished.

South of Fort King, the other attack planned by the Indians was almost over when Thompson was killed.

The army detachment led by Major Francis L. Dade, with eight officers and one hundred enlisted men, was marching along a rough road chopped out of the wilderness. With them was a guide, a black slave named Louis Pacheco.

Pacheco had been born a slave around 1798. He had been owned by a series of army officers until in 1830 he was sold to a Don Antonio Pacheco. On Don Antonio's death a few years later, he became the property of his widow. A valuable slave, priced at $1,000 in 1835, he was described as able-bodied, good-looking, intelligent, able to read and write. He knew four languages: English, Spanish, French, and the Seminole tongue.

When Louis was hired out to the army to guide the troops to Fort King, he knew what their purpose was. He had friends among the Seminole blacks and felt their struggle against the whites was his own. He got word to them of the route he planned to take, where the troops would stop each night, and where best to attack from ambush.

Several Seminole chiefs with their warriors assembled secretly at points along the march. Scouts watched the troops in their sky-blue uniforms every foot of the route and sent reports back to the chiefs. On the morning of the twenty-eighth, Dade's men were advancing in two files through a thin patch of pine woods. It was cold, and the soldiers had their overcoats buttoned over their cartridge boxes. As the advance point of the troops came opposite a pond, the Indians, hidden behind trees, fired upon signal. The storm of bullets brought down Dade and half his men. Louis Pacheco disappeared into the woods and made his way around to the Seminole side. Despite the sudden shock of the attack, the soldiers did not panic. They fell back slowly, firing from behind trees. The Seminole stopped shooting for about an hour, which gave the troops time to pile up a log breastwork. Then the Indians returned to the attack. One by one into the late afternoon the defenders dropped, most of them shot in the head or neck. The wounded were killed as the Indians moved up.

Only one white, left for dead that night, escaped to tell of the massacre. The Indians and blacks lost only three killed and five wounded. Taking food, clothing, and ammunition from the bodies, the warriors stayed that night in the Wahoo Swamp nearby. There they met Osceola, who brought news of the deaths of Thompson and the others at Fort King. They celebrated their success, and next morning woke to learn from scouts that army troops were marching toward the Indian villages on the Withlacoochee. The white force was in two parts: 250 regulars and 500 Florida volunteers. The term of enlistment of the volunteers was to end New Year's Day, and General Clinch had decided to throw them into action before they had to be discharged.

It took the troops three days to reach the Withlacoochee, where, under Osceola's command, 250 warriors, including Abraham with thirty blacks, were lying in wait at the most likely fording place. By chance the troops avoided the ambush, picking a spot to cross two miles above it. The regulars went first in the only canoe available, crossing in sixes and eights to the southern bank where the Indian settlements lay. They rested there, with arms stacked, while the volunteers were still on the northern bank.

Now the Indians, who had moved close, saw the time to attack. From behind scrub timber on the south bank, they fired on the regulars, aiming first for the officers. The shooting went on for an hour, when General Clinch's men made three bayonet charges. After the last, the Seminole withdrew into the swamp, leaving a third of Clinch's men dead or wounded. Most of the volunteers on the other bank had failed to come to the aid of the regulars, either for fear of being killed or because their officers did not order an attack. As darkness came on, Osceola's men returned, and the regulars hurried to recross to the north shore on a hastily erected log bridge.

Shooting from under better cover, the Indians suffered far fewer casualties than the whites. The whites lost four killed and fifty-nine wounded (most of them regulars); the Seminole, three killed and five wounded. The Indians had outmaneuvered the army and prevented a force more than twice their size from reaching the Seminole settlements.

The United States forces took three days to get back to their fort, an agonizing march for the wounded. At once the regulars and the volunteers began to blame each other for the failure at the Withlacoochee. Accusations of malingering, cowardice, and incompetence flew both ways. It was a pattern of charge and countercharge that would recur again and again in this war.

Whoever was at fault, the battle had certain lasting effects. The army mistakenly thought it could get the Seminole to fight in massed attacks, a form of combat the whites were trained in, at which they believed they could beat the Seminole. The Indians gained confidence from their victory, and faith in Osceola's leadership.

With the Battle of the Withlacoochee, it became clear that the United States was in for a serious war. If President Jackson was determined to get the Indians out of Florida and the blacks reenslaved, the price would be great. It would be a sacrifice of blood—not Old Hickory's, but young men's blood.

11

The Balance of Forces

Names like the Withlacoochee meant nothing to the nearly fifteen million people who lived in the United States in 1835. The remote Florida wilderness was a great unknown. The shooting in the swamps echoed only faintly in the nation's press. The people and the politicians were too busy with other matters to take these skirmishes seriously.

They kept their eyes on the main goal—exploiting the great riches of the American continent. In the 1830's, that was much more absorbing than Indian troubles. Speculators traded greedily in public lands. High-profit production of cotton was spreading to the Gulf states. Vast energy and huge sums poured into the building of canals and turnpikes to link the expanding economy. Texas colonists were asserting their right to wrest that empire from Mexico; and the question of Texas raised the issue of slavery. By now the leaders of the anti-slavery cause were publishing dozens of newspapers and organizing hundreds of local chapters throughout the North. The abolitionists protested against annexation as a movement designed to extend slavery.

That slavery had much to do with the war in Florida was not yet clear to most people. They were ignorant of the real causes of the war. The Jacksonian Democrats, very much concerned with defending slavery, gave them little insight into the true nature of the war. The President saw no need for a formal declaration of war against Indians; he was merely putting down a border quarrel.

Jackson was a stubborn, fearless man with a mighty ego. Popular as a military leader, and no less so as President, he acted as though his will were law. He was always ready to resort to violence against anyone who thwarted or opposed him; and his personal character inevitably affected his political behavior. The contempt he showed for authority and law, as in his earlier invasion of Florida, was displayed many times in the White House.

The Seminole could expect no help from him. He did not understand them or care for the justice of their claims. Irritated by their resistance, he simply asked Congress for the funds to carry on hostilities, and ordered troops into the field, no doubt regretting that he could not be there himself.

The United States army at that time was far smaller in power than the nation it served. There were some seven thousand men and six hundred officers scattered about the country on small posts. Their chief was

Major General Alexander Macomb, but Indian wars, unlike foreign wars, were considered beneath his notice. So the Seminole problem was put in the hands of Jackson's Secretary of War, Lewis Cass.

Now in his early fifties, Cass was a fat man with sour mouth, drooping jowls, and icy eyes. He had long been involved in Indian removal. He shaped one of the first experiments—transplanting Oneidas from New York to Wisconsin. As governor of the Michigan Territory for twenty years, he had been in charge of encouraging Indians to get out and whites to come in. He negotiated a score of treaties with Northwest tribes in which they gave up millions of acres. And he posed always as the kind white father who knew what was best for his children. As he once put it, "we must frequently promote their interest against their inclination."

By the time Harvard awarded him an honorary doctor of laws degree in 1836, he was considered the foremost expert on the American Indian. In reality, as his writings show, to him the Indians were not people, not human, but faceless savages. In all his years of experience, he saw them only as "wandering hordes of barbarians" who "cannot live in contact with a civilized community." Therefore they had to be removed.

It should be easy, he thought, to "root the Indians out of their swamps." The Seminole were only so many pesky flies sitting on the flank of the great United States. A flick of the tail and they would be whisked off.

The army called upon to do the job was led by

officers drawn mostly from the West Point military academy. They thought of themselves as an elite few who fought for the honor and glory of their country. The enlisted men they led were at the opposite pole of society: uneducated, outcasts, the dregs of life. A great many were foreigners (almost half of those killed in the Dade massacre were), adrift in the turbulent New World and clinging to the army as a raft. They were an undisciplined lot who drank heavily and deserted easily. Their pay was miserable: five dollars a month—when even a semi-skilled laborer outside drew a dollar a day. Their principal weapon was the muzzle-loaded flintlock, a musket that could hit hard for only a hundred yards. The army's newer rifles were good for four hundred yards, but few were available in the Seminole War.

The navy, too, was small in those times. In Florida, it would be called upon heavily. It had some 750 officers and 4,800 enlisted men, with a marine corps adding another 1,400. A frigate and four sloops of war made up the West Indies Squadron; which bore the brunt of naval service against the Seminole.

None of the United States forces was properly prepared for the kind of war that would develop in Florida. The infantry manual was adapted from the French army's. It had no connection with Indian fighting and nothing to do with Florida climate and terrain.

The Seminole lacked the organization of the American army and were far weaker in numbers. There were perhaps four thousand Seminole, all told, in Florida.

But only about fifteen hundred of them were warriors. The rest were women, children, and old men unfit to fight. Knowing how small the foe's forces were, everyone in Washington expected an easy victory. "The miserable creatures," said a leading newspaper, *Niles' National Register*, "will be speedily swept from the face of the earth."

John Eaton, now governor of the Florida Territory, wasn't so sure. He knew the Seminole will to resist. Do it right, he urged Jackson. Send down an overpowering force—four or five thousand regulars—if you mean to end this war speedily. But to send a giant to swat a gnat? Ridiculous, thought Jackson. The old Indian fighter knew better.

The Indians were equipped with rifles made by the Spanish in Cuba. The trouble with them was their small caliber. The bullets were not big enough to inflict casualties unless primed with the right powder charge. If carelessly loaded, they weren't dangerous beyond twenty yards. The Seminole were said to be careful with the first shot, but not when the firing continued.

The Indians also fought with bow and arrow, as well as knife and hatchet. They wore no uniforms. Some fought only in loincloth and war paint. Others wore traditional feathers and metal ornaments, or parts of uniforms captured from the whites. Their war cry, uttered when they fired a shot, began deep like a growl and ended in a skin-crawling shriek.

Allied with the Seminole force were about three hundred black fighters. They had long before established their reputation as brave warriors. In 1812 a major of the Georgia militia had said of the Seminole that the blacks were "their best soldiers." In addition to the blacks who lived among them, the Seminole could look for support to the plantation slaves and the free blacks. East Florida, where much of the war would be fought, had about 4,000 slaves and 350 free blacks. Together they equaled the number of whites. The slaves as well as the freemen were armed with their own guns for hunting. Many of the slaves had been "sold down the river" to Florida by planters in the upper South who had found them too rebellious; no wonder the Florida whites feared what they might do when war broke out.

The ability of the Seminole to keep their resistance alive so long stemmed in part from the great advantage they could take of a battleground familiar only to them. Florida's terrain and climate favored the Seminole. The whites knew almost nothing about the territory when the war began, not even its actual size. No white had ever seen the whole peninsula. Maps had its rough outline correct, but guessed at the interior or left it blank. The one feature they did show was the fantastic Everglades, the swamp that spread over much of the southern quarter of Florida. But there were other great swamps, where the Seminole fought, and no white man could make his way in them without a red or black guide.

Humped shapes like islands looming out of the saw grass of the swamps were another feature of the landscape. They were called "hammocks," from an Arawak word for masses of vegetation afloat on a river. Up from their rocky depths grew large or small jungles in a thousand tangled forms of tree and blossom. The other terrain the whites had to learn was the sandy barrens from which sprang great pine forests.

It was a wilderness the white army faced, a wilderness whose every swamp and hammock might be a secret citadel for the Seminole. It was a country whites had never explored, a country that offered the invader no roads, bridges, subsistence, or transportation to ease his way.

This, then, was the balance of forces as the Seminole War began. The United States had vastly superior power to draw upon—in men, money, equipment. The Seminole and their black allies were pitifully few, but they were fighting on ground they knew intimately. They were defending their homeland, their independence, their freedom.

Their enemy's only motive was greed for land and greed for slaves.

12

An Unromantic War

News of Dade's disaster and the fighting on the Withlacoochee moved northward slowly. Before Washington woke up to it, sixteen more plantations on the east coast of Florida had been ravaged. Refugees from the countryside crowded into St. Augustine as the town prepared for an assault. The terrified whites cried for help to save them from "butchery by the Indian Negroes." That plea roused volunteer soldiers from Georgia to South Carolina, who came feeling like knights in shining armor, sworn to protect white folks from "the dark demons of ruin," as one of the volunteers put it. The green troops swiftly learned how unromantic war was in the Florida wilderness. By January's end, Seminole warriors had forced the whites to quit the peninsula south of St. Augustine.

It takes money to fight a war. Jackson's Administration had to get the funds from Congress. To pass on the bad news from Florida would mean confessing that the Indian-removal plan had failed. What the opponents of the removal bill of 1830 had predicted had come to pass. Jackson could not keep the promise that force would not be used. Hoping to damp down criticism, he asked for only $80,000. But Congressman Samuel F. Vinton of Ohio would not rubberstamp even that small appropriation. What caused this war and who started it, he demanded to know.

This is no time to raise questions or start debates, Administration stalwarts replied. We're at war and the troops need help. But within days, as more bad news reached the capital, the sum demanded was raised to $500,000. An angry Henry Clay struck out at Jackson:

> It was a condition, altogether without precedent, in which the country was now placed. A war was raging with the most rancorous violence within our borders; congress has been in session nearly two months, during which time this conflict was raging; yet of the causes of the war, how it was produced, if the fault was on one side or on both sides, in short, what had lighted up the torch, congress was altogether uninformed.

In the end, even the enemies of the Administration and the opponents of the Indian-removal policy voted the war funds. Reluctantly, regretfully—still, they went along.

With every dispatch from Florida it became clearer that the Seminole were not going to be put down swiftly or easily. From President Jackson came a volley of orders. Southern governors were asked to furnish militia and volunteers. Arsenals and depots were told to rush arms south. Major General Winfield Scott was posted to Florida to take command. The personal touch of Jackson, the old Indian fighter and slaveholder, is evident in the orders given Scott. One: he was not to offer any terms to the Seminole so long as one white man's slave remained among them. Two: he was not to treat with the Indians until he had first forced them into unconditional surrender.

Scott, at fifty, was a huge man who loved to display his six feet four inches in brilliant uniforms. He had proved his leadership in the War of 1812; but this was not to be a war fought by rusty rules from European drill manuals. Scott had no experience of Indian fighting and, when he came to taste it in Florida, found it unappetizing. He frowned on the rough dress of the volunteers from out of the fields and woods. His own style was regal: he entered the Florida swamps with band playing and wagons bringing up comfortable furniture and good food and wine. It did not help that he got on badly with the two other generals in his command, Edmund Gaines and Duncan Clinch.

Gaines was commander of the army's Western department. The line dividing it from the Eastern command ran right through the war zone. When news reached Gaines of the trouble in Florida, he was at New Orleans. As fast in response as Scott was ponderous, he went at once by sea to Tampa Bay and with almost a thousand troops headed north for Fort King. There he found only a small part of the huge supplies

Scott had ordered. Unable to equip his army properly, he turned back toward Tampa. This meant he would enter the battleground set aside for General Clinch by Scott in his master campaign plan. That plan called for three columns to drive southward through Indian country to a meeting point at the Cove of the Withlacoochee. Here the Seminole's main body of warriors was reported to be concentrated. And here Scott hoped to smash them and end the war in one blow.

A day out of Fort King, Gaines's men reached the Withlacoochee, close to Clinch's region. The Seminole, who had watched the troops move north, attacked Gaines as soon as he reached the river crossing. For seven hours they kept up their fire, until the general threw up a log breastwork. Sheltering behind it that night, Gaines sent a message to Clinch: hit the Indians hard, he said, while I hold them together here.

All the next day Seminole bullets splintered the improvised log fort from three sides. Scott's report had been accurate: almost the whole force of Seminole fighters—1,100 men—had joined in the attack. Day after day dragged by and no relief came. Their food supplies gone, the men ate all their horses and mules. Gaines never tried to break out, however. Later he said that if he had driven the Indians off, it would have spoiled Clinch's chance to crush them.

By the eighth day of the siege, five of Gaines's men had been killed, forty-six wounded, and the rest, starving, were too weak to fight. The Seminole must have thought this was the moment to try to reach an agreement. If they wiped out Gaines's forces, they would only rouse American determination to annihilate the Seminole. But with the enemy before them weak and starving, maybe they could negotiate a reasonable agreement. Proposing a truce, they sent in Osceola, Alligator, Jumper, and the two black leaders, Abraham and Caesar, to talk. They offered to lift the siege and withdraw south of the river if the general guaranteed that they could remain there in peace. Gaines replied that he hadn't the power to grant this but would present their proposals to the proper authority. Just then, Clinch's men marched up. Not realizing a truce talk was in progress, they fired on the Indians. Almost at once, the Seminole disappeared into the woods.

A "victory"—that was what Gaines claimed for himself. The war's over now, he said, and left Florida.

Scott, furious at Gaines's interference, went ahead with his master plan. He himself joined the right wing on their march to the rendezvous. When they reached the Withlacoochee, Scott gave the order to strike up the band so that the tired troops could be entertained at their evening meal. The Indians added the zing of bullets that killed two soldiers. Scott was upset; in his book, this simply was not done. One did not fire at the enemy until he had presented himself for battle. The Indians had no such gentlemanly concept of war.

Scott waited for the other two wings to converge, but they never got within thirty miles of each other. Each of the three columns had to make its way into a wilderness where weather and water levels changed the routes from hour to hour. Every kind of trouble had arisen—shortage of supplies, difficulties with transport, incompetence and inefficiency of regulars and volunteers, conflicts between commanders.

The Seminole never struck in strength at any of Scott's wings because the force against them was too overwhelming. Instead, they took bites out of the edges, wearing the troops down by surprise skirmishes, causing casualty after casualty. Now and then cannon and a bayonet charge scattered the Seminole, but the Indians never did let themselves be enticed into a frontal battle. Finally, the three columns arrived at Fort Brooke, all in a sad state. They had killed fewer than sixty Indians and, instead of destroying a massed force, had succeeded in doing just the opposite. They had split the Seminole into smaller and more effective fighting units of two hundred men or less. Scott's army was crippled by hunger and sickness and worn out by weather and rough use.

His grand plan was a failure. Scott blamed it on the volunteers. It will take three thousand troops to end this war, he told Washington, and they should be "good troops"—not volunteers. He had a bitter word too for the panicky white citizens of Florida. They saw nothing but Indians behind every bush, he charged, and they fled without bothering to find out whether they ran from squaws or from warriors. The Floridians denied it, of course, and eased their hurt by hanging the general in effigy.

Jackson got rid of Scott and salved his injured feelings with a new assignment. The government sent him to Alabama, where war with the Creeks had broken out again. In his place, Jackson put an old crony, Richard Keith Call. Only a few months before, Call had been made governor of the Florida Territory. Now he combined his civil post with command of a field army. His first task was to pick up the pieces left by Scott and mold them into a fighting force. He had a thousand regulars and 230 volunteers to begin with.

Congress had learned how foolish it was to enlist volunteers for only three months—such an army melted away before it scarcely reached the battlefield—and now it had stretched the term of enlistment to six or twelve months. It also removed a source of resentment by granting volunteers in federal service the same pay and disability benefits as regular soldiers were entitled to. Finally, Congress provided for adding another regiment of dragoons to the army.

Call increased his fighting strength with volunteers from Georgia, Alabama, and Tennessee and succeeded in recruiting some Indians too. In Alabama, Creek chiefs signed a contract to furnish men for service until the Seminole should be conquered. In addition to soldiers' pay, they were to get "such plunder as they may take from the Seminoles." The contract was framed by order of General Thomas Jesup and approved by Secretary of War Lewis Cass. Everyone understood that by "plunder" was meant that the Creeks could take as slaves all the blacks they might capture.

Thus, the American democracy was reverting to the

ancient practice of enslaving individuals captured in war. The people were being taxed to this end, and their army, aided by mercenaries, was carrying out the policy—despite the existence of United States laws against piracy and against the slave trade.

Call also found seventy-five Seminole to serve him as guides. They came from a group of 450 who had all along accepted the removal policy and who were now gathered at Fort Brooke on Tampa Bay awaiting shipment to the West.

As a new commander—and one without West Point credentials or even a United States commission—Call sought to show the country at once that he knew how to suppress the Seminole. Congress cheered him on by adding another million and a half dollars to the war budget. His plan was to drive the Seminole beyond the Withlacoochee.

But a Florida summer was a poor time to try for a racing start. And this one of 1836 was one of the worst. Fever overcame the troops by the hundreds. One fort after another in the interior had to be abandoned because so many companies were no longer fit to fight. Wagon trains moving supplies from one point to another were ambushed by the Indians. After one day's march in fiery heat and burning sands, foot soldiers could go no farther. The weather, the fever, and constant harassment by the Indians drove two officers to suicide. By mid-August, white settlers, left unprotected, had deserted the interior. Crammed together in a few villages, housed in miserable shacks, dozens died of measles and diarrhea. Before the summer was over, the Indians found themselves in control of the whole peninsula south of Black Creek and west of the St. Johns. If the whites can do no better than this, they may have thought, perhaps we have a chance.

Call, sick himself that summer, saw nothing come of his campaign plan. Now he looked to its fulfillment in the fall. He, too, hoped to find and destroy the main body of Seminole near the Cove of the Withlacoochee. Along the river were small villages and plantations where the families of many Seminole blacks lived. The crops they had raised during the season were stored on islands in the swamps. Call wanted to devastate the villages and take the supplies.

The volunteer brigade from Tennessee arrived in September. They found Florida "swampy, hammocky, low, excessively hot," as a young lieutenant noted in his diary. In October, Call's forces reached the east bank of the Withlacoochee but were held back from crossing the river by hot fire from the west bank. The general advanced north along the river's edge, but his army soon ran out of food. About six hundred of his horses died for lack of forage. Call could not find the supply depot he was looking for and had to turn back. His score was zero: not once had he had a major battle with the enemy.

Again Call started for the Withlacoochee. This time his Tennessee volunteers, Florida militia, and regulars had the support of 750 Creek fighters, eager to capture blacks whom they could sell as slaves. On

November 13 the army of 2,500 men reached the Withlacoochee. Now they crossed the river without opposition and marched to the heart of the Cove—only to find it abandoned. Not one Seminole—man, woman, or child. Only emply log villages, which Call burned down in a rage. He was a month too late. He had failed again.

The general split his forces in two and swept the territory southward toward the place where Dade had been killed. There was fighting along the way but never a mass engagement. That chance came on November 21 when scouts detected a large concentration of the Seminole in Wahoo Swamp, close by the Withlacoochee. Call sent his entire army into the attack along a mile-wide front. The troops came in shooting on the run, and the Indians returned the fire, but giving ground, so that the army was drawn into the tangled growth of the swamp. After struggling through mud and water two to three feet deep for a mile and a half, the troops reached a running stream about ten yards wide. They hesitated, for the black swamp water looked deep. Across the bank, from behind logs and stumps, the Seminole laid down a withering fire. Although outnumbered four to one—their force counted about 420 Indian and 200 black warriors—the Seminole, defending their families and homes behind them, held off the enemy. One of their most conspicuous leaders, a black, was recognized by the Florida militiamen as the missing property of a planter. A runaway slave directing men in combat? It gave the whites something more to worry about.

The army officers conferred on whether to force a crossing of the creek and make a bayonet charge. They decided against it. They feared the water was too deep (later they learned it was only three feet), their supplies were low, and night was coming on fast. So they withdrew.

"A brilliant day," wrote Colonel B. K. Pierce in his report, "resounding to the honor of our arms, and calculated to bring the war to a speedy termination."

It was a hollow claim. The first year of the war was ending in a complete failure for the United States. The Seminole were still in the field, and still resisting.

13

The General's Treachery

The third general to take command in Florida was another of Jackson's favorites, Thomas Sidney Jesup, a Virginian. He too had fought in the War of 1812 and risen rapidly to become quartermaster general at the age of thirty. Now, at fifty-eight, he had attained the rank of major general and a mixed reputation. Capable, yes, but some accused him of being shifty, a man of bad faith. Fresh from fighting the Creeks in Alabama, he received orders to attack the Seminole and drive them from the region between Tampa Bay and the Withlacoochee.

From the moment he arrived in Florida early in December 1836, Jesup determined to move fast. Speed was vital because the force he took over from Richard Call consisted mostly of citizen soldiers whose enlistments would soon be up.

Scouts told Jesup that Seminole bands under Osceola, Micanopy, Philip, and Cooper were hardly a day's march from one another. Each was said to have from 120 to 200 red and black warriors, with the latter probably more numerous.

This last fact—the major role blacks were playing in the war—led the new commander to add in his report that "this, you may be assured, is a Negro, not an Indian war; and if it be not speedily put down, the south will feel the effects of it on their slave population before the end of the next season."

The whites along the St. Johns already knew what that meant. John Caesar, the Seminole black, had been leading guerrilla raids on their plantations. His men were mostly runaway slaves whose rebellious fires he had fanned on this same plantation belt early in the war. In mid-January he struck within two miles of St. Augustine, trying to take off horses for his men. Discovered by a sentinel, his band was driven off. A troop from the town traced them and late that night attacked the guerrilla camp. They killed Caesar, another Seminole black, and a free black who had joined them six weeks before.

The nine survivors fled, but the supplies and equipment they had to leave behind showed they had had the cooperation of St. Augustine's black population. With this discovery, the panic felt by the whites at the beginning of the war flared up again. Runaway slaves were still at large. What bloody insurrection might they be plotting with their fellows inside the town? The militia were ordered to stick close by. No matter that Jesup was calling for them.

The new commander was shrewd and aggressive. He

had learned the lesson of the expeditions to the Wahoo Swamp. There was no sense to massing troops, on horse or foot, in the enemy's country, without a base of operations. It would only cost lives and gain nothing. More, it encouraged the Indians to think they could win.

No, Jesup would not try to crush the Seminole on the battleground. His policy was to track them down and capture them in their camps. He itched to get his hands on their women and children. Then he could barter their lives for surrender of the warriors. Believing the black resistance was the key to this war, he thought raiding the black villages and breaking their will to fight would be the best way to achieve his end. And to help him he could count on the Creek warriors, who had been promised all the blacks they could capture.

In his first month, the general's troops raked through the swamps, burning villages and driving east the reds and blacks they did not kill or capture. Near the Withlacoochee, the troops had their greatest success. They ferreted out Osceola's headquarters at a black village in a swamp. Though sick, the chief managed to get away with three warriors. But fifty-two blacks and three Indians, mostly women and children, were taken prisoner. Soon Jesup could count 131 captives—these, too, mostly black women and children.

The Seminole warriors—red and black—moved toward the head of the Caloosahatchee. The army pursued them, catching up with the baggage train and taking about twenty prisoners, again black women and children. There was some fighting in the Great Cypress Swamp, with a few casualties on both sides. But "not a single first-rate warrior had been captured, and only two Indian men have surrendered," Jesup lamented in a report. "The warriors have fought as long as they had life, and such seems to me to be the determination of those who influence their councils—I mean the leading Negroes."

He could scour the swamps endlessly for Seminole, and come out with only these small prizes. Jesup began to think there must be a better way to end the war. There were more minor skirmishes, more women and children captured, and still the warriors got away. "If I have at any time said aught in disparagement of the operations of others in Florida," Jesup confided to a friend, "I consider myself bound, as a man of honor, solemnly to retract it."

Now he ordered troops to move in any direction, wherever he heard there might be bands of Seminole. Still, no conclusive battles. One day in January, however, a captured black named Ben, one of Micanopy's men, told Jesup's officers that Jumper and Abraham were nearby and would come in to talk if guaranteed their safety. Ben was sent back to the Seminole with hints of a liberal treaty. A few days later Abraham arrived with Jumper, Alligator, and John Cavallo, a black subchief.

Why would the Indians want to do this? By now they must have realized there was no future in this kind of war. They were being hunted like wolves through the peninsula; their families were forever forced to move to avoid capture or death; all of them faced constant hunger. It was a stupid war whose continuation would gain them nothing. If they resisted to the end, they would surely almost all die or be enslaved. If they tried to make a treaty with a foe that was as sick of the fighting as they were, then maybe they could get decent terms, terms they could live with honorably. Abraham especially saw how impossible it was to live decently in Florida when the government was grimly set on driving them out. Now, he felt, the time was ripe to talk.

On March 6, 1837, after a month's negotiations at Camp Dade, a treaty was concluded. Jesup and the Seminole chiefs agreed to stop the fighting. The Indians promised to come to Tampa Bay by April 10, and board the ships for the West. The whites would support the Seminole from the time they turned themselves in till they arrived at their new homes, and for a year thereafter. Hostages would be given to the whites to back up the Indians' promises.

Jesup, most significantly, agreed to the major condition the Seminole had insisted upon from the start: "The Seminoles, and their allies, who come in and emigrate west, shall be secure in their lives and property"; and "their Negroes, their bona fide property, shall accompany them to the West." So the signed agreement read. It was headed, "Capitulation of the Seminole nation of Indians and their allies . . ."

Jesup was confident that this agreement would guarantee the removal of the Seminole if he could keep the support of the blacks. "It is important that they should feel themselves secure," he said. "If they should become alarmed and hold out, the war will be renewed." That was why the document made a point of the Seminole's "allies," meaning the free blacks, who were assured their life and property. It also guaranteed that those blacks who were the property of the Indians would go west with their masters. Abraham, speaking for the Seminole blacks, wanted that assurance. So did the army, for it knew that if the blacks were assured their safety from slaveholders, the blacks would no longer be a barrier to Seminole migration.

But the fact that this was a war to catch slaves as well as to drive out Indians was to destroy Jesup's hopes. The Florida whites did not want any part of this treaty. Neither did any slaveholder. It's just as important that we get our slaves back as that the country find peace, they said. Where is the clause to indemnify us for the slaves taken by the Seminole? How can the government let all these blacks leave Florida when every damn one of them belongs rightfully to some white master?

Florida editorials cursed out Jesup as though he were an abolitionist. His only aim was to carry out his orders and get the Seminole out of Florida. If doing that meant that the blacks had to go with them, then so be it.

The slaveholders would not have it that way. Already their agents had shown up in camp to claim this black or that who had surrendered. Alarmed, the blacks began to flee. Jesup swiftly moved the others to a safer place, fearful that the war would start up all over again.

Under pressure from greedy slaveowners, the general began to lean the other way. Maybe he should draw the line between those blacks who had lived with the Seminole before the war and those who had run off to them or been picked up by them during the war. He began to urge the Indians to accept this distinction and hand over all the wartime runaway slaves.

At the same time, he told the whites the Seminole had no obligation to surrender fugitives because the government had provided $7,000 to settle all such claims against them. No, he proclaimed, "I will not make Negro-catchers of the army." But only yesterday he had enlisted the Creeks as "Negro-catchers."

In April, Jesup made a secret deal with Coa Hadjo and some other chiefs. They were to hand over all blacks who had joined them since the outbreak of the war. Some blacks were given up, and some, tired of the hardships of a guerrilla war, came in on their own. Others were determined to resist. A band of blacks on Cedar Creek defied Coa Hadjo's attempt to send them back to the whites. He had not captured them, they said, and he would never return them.

Such blacks had the backing of Osceola. Not a Seminole chief by birth, he found his following among the volunteers. Runaway slaves were drawn to his courage and intelligent leadership. Although there were militant Mikasukis in his band, his fighters were mostly the fugitive blacks. When Coa Hadjo stood up in council to propose that runaways be returned, Osceola angrily denounced the change in policy. So long as he was in the nation, he said, it would never be done.

In June, Jesup tried to induce the Florida militia to fight harder by offering the lure of black booty. He wrote their commander: "There is no obligation to spare the property of the Indians. . . . Their Negroes, cattle and horses . . . will belong to the corps by which they are captured." Creek and white troops were already busy hunting down blacks. They brought in 125 they called slaves; 35 were given to white claimants; and the remaining 90 were sent to Fort Pike in New Orleans. Jesup reported: "The Seminole Negro prisoners are now the property of the public. . . . The Creek Indians were entitled to all the Indian property they captured. I compromised with them by purchasing the Negroes from them on account of the government, for which I agreed to pay them eight thousand dollars. . . . I was also compelled to pay the Indians a reward of twenty dollars each for the Negroes captured by them, the property of citizens."

So Jesup had made the government itself the owner of slaves. He bought the Seminole blacks from the Creeks because, according to the historian Kenneth W. Porter, he wanted "to prevent the dissemination among plantations in the Deep South of Negroes accustomed to freedom and trained in the use of arms, who might take the lead in slave insurrections." Jesup wrote Washington: "It is highly important to the slaveholding

States that these Negroes be sent out of the country, and I would strongly recommend that they be sent to one of our colonies in Africa."

But the Creeks saw a better business deal elsewhere. Instead of accepting the $8,000, they sold the ninety black captives to a Georgia slave trader for about $15,000.

That April and May, many important Seminole leaders with their followers began assembling near Tampa, as though preparing to emigrate. Osceola was among them, and Philip and his son Caocoochee, Sam Jones, Coa Hadjo, Yaholocoochee. Still, only a few came to the point of embarkation in Tampa. Army officers began to feel that the Indians were stalling while living on government rations.

Jesup, restless, angry, sent a threat to Osceola that bloodhounds from Cuba would be unleashed against the holdouts and the captured Indians would be hanged if the delay continued. Soon Alligator, Jumper, Cloud, and Micanopy came into the detention camp.

Jesup began to feel more optimistic. Then suddenly, the night of June 2, a band of two hundred warriors led by Osceola, Sam Jones, Caocoochee, and John Cavallo filtered quietly into the detention camp and, despite the sentinels, led out every Seminole who had been held inside. About seven hundred people slipped out of Jesup's grasp. "All is lost," he moaned, "and principally by the influence of the Negroes."

This kidnapping-with-consent-of-the-kidnapped exploded Jesup's peace plan. If he had lived up to the

March 6 agreement, this might not have happened. But when Jesup began to betray his pledge to honor the ties between red and black, the fighting was bound to start again. It is also true that the younger chiefs, such as Osceola, seemed determined never to leave their country.

Savagely criticized on all sides, Jesup turned bitter and cynical. At first he wanted to see no more of Florida. But by the time Washington offered to let him withdraw from command, he had changed his mind. Now he felt the Seminole had betrayed *him*. If they did not keep their promises, he was ready to use treachery to win.

So he stayed. His new plan was the old strategy of divide and conquer. He tried to split the Seminole—dividing the Alachua from the more militant Mikasukis and Tallahassees. That failed. Then he tried to split the blacks from the reds. What gave him this idea was the news that some of the runaway slaves were slipping away from the Seminole and going back to the plantations. After twenty months of hardship in combat, over fifty of the fugitives from the St. Johns region, close to starvation, had decided to swap freedom for food. Among them was John Philip, a slave of Chief Philip.

Another reason for the black defeatism may have been the great loss in leadership suffered when several of their outstanding men were taken into custody after the capitulation at Fort Dade. Among the hundred Seminole blacks held by Jesup were a score of warriors, including Abraham and three other chiefs. John Caesar, too, was gone, killed in action. "The Negro portion of the hostile forces of the Seminole nation not taken is entirely without a head," Jesup reported. The bands of black fighters, their chiefs gone, seemed to be drifting away from the Indians.

Jesup seized the opening. He put out offers of freedom and safety to blacks if they would leave the Seminole. More and more blacks took up his offer and came in, most of them reported to be "in starving condition." Jesup had no legal power to grant many of them the freedom he promised. Those who could be proved to be the property of whites could be reclaimed as slaves. But Jesup tried to keep his promise. He treated these blacks as the property of the Seminole, so that under the March 6 treaty he could ship them west with the Indians.

It was a way of saying that the government would safeguard the freedom the blacks had known with the Seminole, something the Indians could no longer do. The policy later was extended to all blacks captured or surrendered. They were sent across the Mississippi into Indian Territory no matter when or how they had joined the Indians. It was not out of humanitarian motives that this was done. The army knew that people who had tasted freedom or fought with guns for it, if returned to slavery, would either run away again or stir up revolt.

If a white made a convincing claim for such a black, the army would recommend giving the white compensation and before the case was settled would have shipped the black west out of the claimant's reach. Eventually, all captured blacks were sent west, saved from slavery.

Jesup realized that white settlers were not yet ready to push into southern Florida, so he suggested to Washington that the Seminole be allowed to stay there. The Indians could always be forced to emigrate when their land was needed. But Joel Poinsett, a South Carolinian chosen to be Secretary of War by the new President, Martin Van Buren, flatly refused. If we let the Seminole remain, he said, it will make us appear weaklings to all the other tribes we want to move west. And they too will put up a bloody resistance. No, he told Jesup, keep pushing the Seminole hard, and we'll give you more power to finish the job.

Privately, Jesup said the government policy was "unholy." But he had his duty to perform. He would do what he was ordered to do. He used the summer of 1837 to prepare for a fall campaign. He wished he could rely on regular troops only, but unable to get enough of them, he had to take citizen soldiers. Many of these were newly arrived foreigners, or laborers and mechanics from the cities, left jobless and hungry by the depression that was crippling the country. They did not really want to fight. The army was a temporary shelter to them. If he had to use untrained soldiers, Jesup preferred farm boys. They still responded to patriotic appeals. Dissatisfied with the Creeks—they had lost heart after the battle of the Great Wahoo Swamp, and besides, their families in Alabama were being badly treated in concentration camps—Jesup got permission to recruit other Indians. A band of Delawares and a band of Shawnees were brought east across the Mississippi to enlarge his army.

Jesup was bent on getting more and better equipment for the coming campaign. He secured Dearborn wagons, whose big wheels, wide tires, and watertight bodies made them usable as boats as well. Horses, mules, wagons, packsaddles, river steamers, pontoon boats, Colt revolvers, Cochran repeaters, shotguns, tents of all kinds, hatchets, axes, shovels, rations better suited to Florida's climate—a thousand and one such necessities streamed in all summer long.

Early in September, the campaign began with two quick and easy victories for Jesup. John Philip—whether willingly or under pressure—led white troops to a surprise raid at midnight on King Philip's hidden camp thirty miles south of St. Augustine. A mounted charge captured all but one of the Indians, including King Philip himself. One of the Indians taken, greedy for plunder, offered to guide the troops to the nearby camp of the Yuchis. At dawn, another surprise attack succeeded in capturing the whole band and its chief, Yuchi Billy.

With two important Seminole leaders taken, Jesup's hopes rose. King Philip asked for permission to have his oldest son, Coacoochee—called Wildcat by the whites—visit him in captivity. A runner went out and the son came in under a white flag, accompanied by Blue Smoke. Disregarding one of the most honored rules of war, Jesup took the two Indians prisoner. Using King Philip as hostage, Jesup told the son to go back to the Seminole and bring in more of his followers. Fail to return, he warned, and your father will be killed.

Coacoochee reached Osceola and Coa Hadjo with the message that his father wanted them to come in and hold peace talks. Late in October the two leaders let Jesup know they were ready to do so. The general now prepared a piece of treachery that has dishonored him ever since. Again he decided he would violate a flag of truce. As the first step in the plot, he instructed General Hernandez, a Florida militia commander, to agree to a parley.

The conference was to take place near St. Augustine on October 21. When Hernandez, with 250 mounted troops behind him, came up to the Indian camp, a white flag was flying over it. That was a sign that the meeting was a truce, not a surrender. Under the rules of war, the white flag meant that no injury would be done to anyone.

While Osceola stood by silently, Coa Hadjo spoke for the Seminole. "We want to make peace," he said. The general replied: "We have been deceived so often that it is necessary for you to come with me. . . . You will all see the good treatment that you will experience—you will be glad that you fell into my hands."

Then Hernandez gave a prearranged signal and the white troops closed in on the Indians. So swiftly was it done that the Seminole had no chance to fire.

It was "the most notorious treachery of the Second

Seminole War," in the judgment of Professor Mahon. Jesup captured Osceola, Coa Hadjo, Coacoochee, John Cavallo, and other leaders, as well as seventy-one warriors, six women, and four blacks, together with their weapons.

Escorted by cavalry, the captives were paraded through the streets of St. Augustine while the whole town watched. An army surgeon, Nathan Jarvis, noted that Osceola wore a bright blue calico shirt, red leggings, a print turban, and over his shoulders a vivid shawl. But the chief looked sick, the doctor thought.

The deceit Jesup used to capture Osceola, already a hero to the abolitionists and to those who opposed the Indian-removal policy, excited a terrific uproar. In Washington, *Niles' National Register* wrote: "We disclaim all participation in the 'glory' of this achievement of American generalship. If practiced towards a civilized foe, [it] would be characterized as a violation of all that is noble and generous in war." The storm of disapproval rolled over the floor of Congress, where legislators called Jesup a "villain."

Jesup tried to defend himself—he never stopped till his death many years later—arguing that since the Seminole had broken their promises, there was no reason why the Americans should keep theirs. Besides, he said, breach of faith or not, this was the only way to end the war and save lives on both sides.

The Indians thought the whites' behavior utterly disgraceful. In their own intertribal warfare, they always held ambassadors and a truce sacred. Indians everywhere in the country soon saw, however, that American commanders would use any excuse to arrest Indian negotiators and hold them, regardless of a flag of truce. Jesup was the model of the racist who did not believe the rules of "civilized" warfare applied to "savages." Again and again he would use such treachery to capture Seminole fighters. It became a standard practice of the American military.

Even though they would be deceived time and again, the Seminole continued to come in to negotiate. Did they tell themselves that the *next* time the whites would surely act honorably? Or was it rather, as the historian Dale Van Every suggests, that they came to know their cause was hopeless, and allowing themselves to be captured by treachery was a way to save face?

14

Battles in the Wilderness and in Washington

Osceola was placed in the military prison in St. Augustine that held so many other Seminole taken by the same tactics of deceit. Sick when captured, the Indian rapidly grew worse in confinement. Late in the year General Jesup ordered him sent to Fort Moultrie in Charleston harbor, South Carolina. It is probable that a malarial infection contracted the year before was the cause of Osceola's illness. The effect of the chronic fever was noted by many who had seen him during the previous eighteen months.

At Fort Moultrie, despite his condition, Osceola gave permission for his portrait to be done by George Catlin, an American artist renowned for his superb paintings of Indian life. In January 1838, during the sittings, Osceola suffered a bad sore throat, which grew dangerous because the malaria had lowered his resistance. The post surgeon, Dr. Frederick Weedon, told Catlin that the Seminole would probably not survive the winter.

Weedon was the brother-in-law of Wiley Thompson, the Indian agent Osceola had killed early in the war. Osceola may have known this; he insisted on treatment at the hands of an Indian medicine man.

Toward the end of January, Osceola's strength declined rapidly. His last hours on January 31 were described by Weedon:

About half an hour before he died, he seemed to be sensible that he was dying; and although he could not speak, he signified by signs that he wished me to send for the chiefs and for the officers of the post, whom I called in. He made signs to his wives (of whom he had two, and also two fine little children by his side), to go and bring his full dress, which he wore in time of war; which having been brought in, he rose up in his bed, which was on the floor, and put on his shirt, his leggings and moccasins—girded on his war-belt, his bullet-pouch, and powder-horn, and laid his knife by the side of him on the floor.

He then called for his red paint, and his looking-glass, which was held before him, when he deliberately painted on half of his face, his neck and his throat—his wrists—the backs of his hands, and the handle of his knife, red with vermillion; a custom practiced when the irrevocable oath of war and destruction is taken. His knife he then placed in its sheath, under his belt; and he carefully arranged his turban on his head, and his three ostrich plumes that he was in the habit of wearing in it.

Being thus prepared in full dress, he lay down a few minutes to recover strength sufficient, when he rose up as before, and with most benignant and pleasing smiles, extended his hand to me and to all of the officers and chiefs that were around him; and shook hands with all of us in dead silence; and also with his wives and his little children; he made a signal for them to lower him down upon his bed, which was done, and he then slowly drew from his war-belt, his scalping knife, which he firmly grasped in his right hand, laying it across the other, on his breast, and in a moment smiled away his last breath, without a struggle or a groan.

The doctor did not mention that he then cut off Osceola's head, embalmed it, and kept it in his home. Sometimes he hung it over the bed of one of his children as punishment for misconduct.

Osceola's headless body was buried at Fort Moultrie. One of the Seminole's best leaders was gone. But his death did not end the war. His heroic resistance to the removal policy, his treacherous capture, and his death in prison made him a legendary symbol of men who defend their homeland from invaders.

Shortly after Osceola's capture, a delegation of Cherokees led by John Ross, their principal chief, arrived in St. Augustine after a thousand-mile trip from

Indian Territory. The War Department had enlisted their help in persuading the Seminole to accept removal. The Cherokees' mission was humane: they hoped to avert the further shedding of blood in a cause they believed futile. Ross saw how the prolonged Seminole resistance was brutalizing the whites. He had come to the conviction that nonviolence was the only hope Indians had of achieving any accommodation with the powerful American government. That was why he accepted the invitation to mediate. Jesup, distrusting the Cherokees as much as he did the Seminole, did not welcome their arrival. He was getting ready to fight and did not want to stop for parleys. The Cherokees, accompanied by Coa Hadjo, traveled south to talk with Micanopy. They came back to Jesup with Micanopy and twelve subchiefs, ready to talk.

The general received Micanopy's group coldly. He demanded what amounted to unconditional surrender. They had to give themselves up, bring in their families, and accept the capitulation of March 6. The Cherokees were appalled by Jesup's behavior. He treated Micanopy and his people as though they had come in, not to talk under a flag of truce, but to surrender. And now he held the chiefs as hostages so that their followers would submit. Despite Jesup's behavior, the Cherokees once more set out to persuade other Seminole chiefs to surrender.

This time the delegation had to deal with Seminole leaders much tougher than Micanopy. One of them was Coacoochee, Philip's son. Coacoochee had been among the prisoners taken treacherously with Osceola in October. Confined to the fort at St. Augustine, he and John Cavallo were placed in a cell with many other Seminole. The prison, half decayed, was guarded by poorly paid soldiers who eased their dull lives by getting drunk. The menial chores were done by free blacks or hired slaves. After a month's imprisonment, during which they probably tried and failed to bargain their way out, Coacoochee and John Cavallo plotted an escape. On November 29, in the dark of the moon, one after another the Indians in their cell managed to climb the wall of the cell to reach a small opening high up. Those who were thin enough wriggled through and with a rope made of slit bedding shinnied down the outer wall to a ditch below. Led by Coacoochee and Cavallo, eighteen other Seminole, including two women, made their escape that night. They slipped through the town, forded the river, and traveling by night and sleeping by day in the forest, reached their people to the south.

The successful break for liberty was a bad blow to Jesup, for Coacoochee proved to be of enormous importance to the continuation of the Seminole War. "He was," according to Professor Porter, "the one man capable of assuming leadership over a significant number of the Seminoles and reviving the waning spirit of other chiefs, a man young, vigorous, intelligent, courageous, and with hereditary claims to chieftancy; neither the aged Philip, the indolent Micanopy, the sickly Jumper, the double-dealing Coa Hadjo, the weary Osceola, could have maintained the struggle for more than three years longer with the ability and tenacity displayed by Coacoochee."

When the Cherokees reached Coacoochee with Jesup's call to surrender, the young Seminole leader laughed at them. He had just escaped from the great white general's fortress and was not about to put himself in his power again. Nor was Arpeika. He denounced the Cherokees for playing along with Jesup.

The Cherokees went back to Jesup to report their failure. His response was to ship Micanopy and eighty-one other Indians to St. Augustine as prisoners of war. He turned a deaf ear to the protests of the enraged Cherokees. You are violating the flag of truce the Seminole came in under, they said, and staining Cherokee honor by involving us in your guilt. Jesup did not care. The Cherokee gave up their attempts to mediate and left for the West. At home, John Ross wrote a furious letter to the Secretary of War:

> I do hereby most solemnly protest against the unprecedented violation of that sacred rule which has ever been recognized by every nation, civilized and uncivilized, of treating with all due respect those who had ever presented themselves under a flag of truce before their enemy, for the purpose of proposing the termination of a warfare.

Now, in December, while one stream of Seminole Indians and blacks was moving toward the emigration camp at Tampa Bay, another was heading for the lower

Kissimmee River and Lake Okeechobee, where the die-hards were concentrating to make a stand. In the next month the militants would fight three of the greatest battles of the seven-year war.

As soon as Jesup had made Micanopy his prisoner, he ordered Colonel Zachary Taylor to move out against the Indians. His mission was to conquer or destroy all those who stubbornly refused to give up. Taylor and his First Infantry Regiment had recently joined Jesup's command. Now fifty-three, Taylor had been in the army for thirty years. He too had fought in the War of 1812 and then, a self-educated man, had slowly risen to colonel while on frontier duty. After service in the Black Hawk War, he was ordered to Florida.

Taylor marched out with about a thousand men to hunt the Seminole. Most of his troops were regulars, with some volunteers, plus seventy Delaware and Shawnee Indians who had been offered plunder through the capture of slaves.

Taylor headed south down the Kissimmee toward Lake Okeechobee. He hoped to engage the full force of the enemy. Soon he met Jumper and some sixty of his followers, ready to surrender, and sent them back to the fort under Shawnee guard. On the third day, he left his artillery and heavy baggage in a small stockade because the trail was hard going and he wanted to be able to maneuver rapidly. He felt encouraged when Indians dribbled in to give themselves up. He knew he must be near the enemy's major force. But as he entered a swamp or hammock, the Seminole were always just leaving it on the other side. At last the army reached a large empty camp whose fires were still burning, and captured a lone Seminole probably left there to draw them on.

On Christmas day Taylor's army came up to a large hammock with half a mile of swamp in front of it. On the far side of the hammock was Lake Okeechobee. Here the saw grass stood five feet high. The mud and water were three feet deep. Horses would be of no use. It was plain that the Seminole meant this to be the battleground. They had sliced the grass to provide an open field of fire and had notched the trees to steady their rifles. Their scouts were perched in the treetops to follow every movement of the troops coming up.

About four hundred Indians—less than half the size of Taylor's force—stood ready for battle, shielded behind the thick trees of the hammock. Their right wing was led by Arpeika, the center by Alligator, and the left by Coacoochee. As was their custom, each wing operated on its own, without a unifying central command. Nor did they have the support of any large number of black warriors for this battle.

At half past noon, the sun shining directly overhead, and the air still and quiet, Taylor moved his troops squarely into the center of the swamp. His plan was to make a direct attack, rather than to encircle the Indians. All his men were on foot. In the first line were the Missouri volunteers. As soon as they came within range, the Indians opened with heavy fire. The volunteers broke, and their commander, Colonel Gentry, fatally wounded, was unable to rally them. They fled back across the swamp. The fighting in the saw grass was deadliest for five companies of the Sixth Infantry; every officer but one, and most of their noncoms, were killed or wounded. When that part of the regiment retired a short distance to re-form, they found only four men of these companies unharmed.

With the frontal attack launched, Taylor sent his reserve, the First Infantry, to hit the Seminole on their right flank. As their attack opened, the Indians under Arpeika fired a final volley and began to withdraw under great pressure. About three in the afternoon, the Seminole moved back toward the lake and, scattering, disappeared toward the east. Taylor did not try to follow them. He had too many casualties to take care of.

The Battle of Lake Okeechobee, as it came to be called, was the costliest conflict of the war for the United States. The whites lost 26 killed and 112 wounded: the Seminole, 11 dead and 14 wounded.

Colonel Taylor and his surviving officers, moving about the field to pick up the dead and crippled, could see for themselves the expense of subduing a people fighting for their homes and their freedom. Writing not long after the war, Congressman Joshua Giddings said:

It is one of the imperfections of human government that the men who conceive and direct the perpetration of great national crimes are usually exempt from the immediate dangers which beset those who

> act merely as their instruments in the consummation of transcendent wrongs. Had General Jackson and General Cass been assured they would have been the first individuals to meet death in their efforts to enslave the Exiles [the Seminole blacks], it is doubtful whether either of them would have been willing to adopt a policy which should thus consign them to premature graves. Or had Mr. Van Buren or his Cabinet . . . been conscious that, in carrying out this war for slavery they would fall victim to their own policy, it may well be doubted whether either of them would have laid down his life for the safety of that institution; yet they were evidently willing to sacrifice our military officers and soldiers. . . .

The next action against the Indians took place on January 15, 1838. The Americans, commanded by Lieutenant Levi N. Powell of the navy, were a mixed force of sailors (most of them black), artillery, and volunteer infantry. Their task was to hunt down the Seminole in the Everglades. They had started in boats, but with the temperature soaring over one hundred that season, the boats lacked water to float in and had to be dragged. At Jupiter Inlet on the Atlantic, east of Lake Okeechobee, they charged a camp they spotted through smoke rising from a swamp. But such hot gunfire repelled them that they had to fight a rear-guard action to make it back to their boats. They lost five killed and fifteen wounded.

General Jesup himself was now in the field, directing

several mobile columns in the closing of a ring around the Seminole's southern region. His troops had started to inch their way south on January 3. At noon on the twenty-fourth, scouts reported a body of Indians in a hammock just ahead, close by Jupiter Inlet. Eager to show his mettle in combat, Jesup ordered an immediate attack. The horses foundered in the swamp and the troops had to dismount. They charged in with artillery firing from behind them. When the shooting grew intense, the Indians moved back across a stream about thirty yards wide, and began peppering the Tennessee volunteers on the other side. Seeing the volunteers grow panicky, Jesup rode up and ordered them to advance. A bullet hit his eyeglasses and cut open his cheek. Jesup waved the troops on, retrieved the pieces of his spectacles, and rode to the rear. The Indians gradually melted away, and the whites were left to count their casualties. They lost seven dead and thirty-one wounded in the Battle of the Lockahatchee. The cost to the Seminole, whose force was estimated at two to three hundred, was unknown because they left neither dead nor wounded on the field.

On the very day of this battle, the House of Representatives was debating the Seminole War. The War Department had asked Congress for a partial appropriation of one million dollars to cover some expenses recently incurred in suppressing the Indians. Later the government meant to ask for another $2,480,000 to take care of hostilities in 1838. Charles Downing, delegate from Florida, urged the House to pass the bill without delay. That opened the door to a heated discussion. These excerpts from the *Congressional Globe* reporting the debate reveal a great deal about the division of opinion over the Seminole War:

MR. DOWNING: It was his opinion that this war would be brought to a speedy termination, if the means were put in the hands of the Government for carrying it on; and gentlemen need not be apprehensive of its prolongation. The late efforts made there were decisive, and he believed the war would be brought to a close in a very short time.

MR. WISE (Virginia): It was in this way the appropriations were extracted from this House, like teeth, without the proper investigation and inquiry. The officers of Government waited until appropriations were immediately wanted, and then they called upon the House to pass them, without discussion. In this manner that nine-tenths, if not all of the eight, nine or ten millions of dollars which had been appropriated for this fatal, disastrous, disgraceful Seminole campaign had been obtained. . . . He wished information too, in relation to the perfidy which had been practiced by officers of the army towards these Indians . . . as he believed the greatest outrages had been committed upon them, which was the only reason of the war being kept up. He felt sufficiently humbled by this outrageous and disgraceful war, and he would rather vote to secure those unfortunate Indians in their hammocks than from them.

MR. DOWNING: The gentleman had called it an unfortunate war. So it was. The war had been prolonged beyond the calculation of any human being. But whose fault was it that it had been so prolonged? Was it the fault of the troops engaged in it, or the militia raised for its suppression? No: its prolongation had been caused by the gentleman, and the friends of the gentleman, who now oppose the appropriation. . . . Every officer engaged in the war had acted his part zealously and effectively; but the evil was, that they had to check their efforts, because they were compelled to bend to that sympathy manifested so generally for the "red man" in the North and other portions of the Union, where the true state of things was not known. The only reason that the war was not ended long ago was that the troops had been compelled by that sympathy to hold out the white flag to the "poor devils," to give them time to make peace, when they were entirely in our power. If the people of Florida had heard nothing from the pulpit and the press about the wrongs of the "poor Indians," and such ebullitions of blind feeling, the war would long since have been suspended. Had the people of Florida been permitted to adopt their own measures, and if the rope and the gallows had been used, as they would in the case of white men committing such enormities, the affair would have been settled long before this. . . . But public sentiment and sympathy was ever ready to extend itself for the red man and the Negro. The white men of the South might be butchered by the hundreds, and the act looked upon with indifference; but when colored skins were concerned, then it was that an outcry was raised. It was for the Indians and the Negro for whom the public sympathy boiled and bubbled over. . . .

There were more exchanges between the congressmen, with Downing complaining that the Seminole "were just like a flea, the moment a man put his hand upon one, thinking he had caught him, that instant it would be in some other place." He drew a comparison between the leader of the Virginia slave uprising of 1831, Nat Turner, who had concealed himself in the Dismal Swamp, and the Florida Indians. He then said many people were pressing to let the Indians stay on their territory, and to free their slaves. But the citizens of Florida, he said, "would never submit to such dictation; for the people of Florida would *not* free their slaves, neither would they allow the Indians to remain among them."

Mr. Wise said that if the House would give him a committee of investigation he could prove the charges of fraud made by the Indians.

MR. WISE: He expressed his surprise that the gentleman from Florida had never heard the fairness of the Seminole treaty questioned, for it had been described as a fraud upon that floor a year ago. It had never been ratified by the Indians, and was no more a valid treaty than was the Cherokee treaty.

MR. DOWNING explained that he would not take the testimony of Indians or Negroes in opposition to that of white people; and the validity of the treaty had never been questioned in Florida.

MR. WISE said that he would take the testimony of the Government, of our own agents and our own people, and their testimony was that the treaty had not been fairly obtained, and that it was never made with the Seminole nation, as a nation. In making treaties with the Indians, they are to be heard, as well as ourselves. . . . He [Mr. Wise] had voted time after time, and year after year, for appropriations to suppress these Indian hostilities, without inquiry, until the amount of money struck him with surprise, and he was compelled to pause and inquire into the matter. He considered it a public duty that he should do so, after eight or nine millions had been expended, and troop after troop had been defeated, and the Indians, although but a handful at first, still remained masters of the soil. What a spectacle we were presenting to the world! This Government . . . with all her surplus millions, her regular troops, her marines, her chosen Tennessee troops, and all her militia, could not put down some eight hundred or a thousand Indians. It was impossible for the gentleman to defend the War Department after such management as it had been guilty of, and he contended that that department was responsible for the act of every one of its agents, whether petty or important agents. He went on to charge perfidy and treachery upon the officers of the Government, in seizing upon Osceola and Micanopy, while they were under the white flag which ought to have protected them. . . .

MR. CILLEY defended the policy of the Government, which, he insisted, was humane and benevolent. The sympathy evinced for the tawny red man he described to be of the same character as the hobby professed for the race a little darker in the North. When he found his country at war, he was not for staying to inquire into its origin, or to investigate little, petty, miserable details about it, but to take such measures as would be most likely to bring it to a favorable termination. Whether the Government had pursued the best course or not, whether there had been a prodigal expenditure, he feared there had, he could not say, but he was for continuing the war with vigor, on the old New England plan, where the Indians had been wholly exterminated, for it was false policy and false philanthropy to carry on a feeble war.

MR. EVERETT avowed himself unwilling to carry on this war any longer, though he was not for yielding. He wished a pacificatory course to be tried. He would arm the Executive with authority and appropriations to enable him to adopt a course which should terminate it pacifically.

When the debate ended, all the money the government requested was granted.

Having lost so many men in three costly battles, Jesup considered what to do next. His officers urged him to try to end the war through a treaty that would let the Seminole remain in the southern part of Florida. The general tested the idea by inviting the chiefs to a conference. On February 8 the parley was held. Jesup told Tuskegee and Halleck Hajo he would urge Washington to let the Seminole remain in southern Florida. It was agreed the Seminole should make camp near the fort, where they would be safe, until the government replied. About 550 Seminole, 150 of them blacks, hearing of the possibility of peace on the basis of remaining in Florida, came to the camp near Fort Jupiter.

Jesup wrote to Secretary of War Poinsett. Again he made out a case for holding up on removal of the Indians. Never before, he said, had Indians been forced out of territory before whites needed it. "We have committed the error of attempting to remove them when their lands were not required for agricultural purposes; when they were not in the way of the white inhabitants; and when the greater portion of their country was an unexplored wilderness, of the interior of which we were as ignorant as of the interior of China."

(The war, he was admitting, was not so much for land as for slavery.)

The Seminole have now been pushed to the southern part of the peninsula, he continued, where no whites as yet want to settle. Why not let them stay there, on a reservation? If the government insists on their immediate removal, then the war could drag on for years and years. Our national honor is not at stake, he pointed out. The Seminole are as beaten as any Indians General Jackson ever fought. Do what I ask now, he said. "It is the only means of terminating, immediately, a most disastrous war. . . ."

General Jesup was now recommending the very policy which the Indians and blacks from the beginning had been ready to accept. He had also once said that the subjection of the Seminole was something the army could easily do. His letter must have astonished the War Department.

While both sides awaited word from Washington, Jesup invited the Seminole to visit his camp. The Indians and blacks appeared in ceremonial dress. Army Surgeon Jacob Rhett Motte, like the other officers present, was upset by the blacks' behavior. They are "diabolical looking," he noted in his journal, "ferocious and oriental in aspect. They had none of the servility of our northern blacks, but were constantly offering their dirty paws with as much hauteur and nonchalance as if they were conferring a vast deal of honor." The Seminole in turn invited the officers to attend an Indian dance, and the two enemies got drunk together on whiskey furnished by the whites.

A month later Poinsett's reply arrived. It was a flat refusal to let the Seminole stay. "Put it out of the power of these Indians to do any further mischief. They ought to be captured or destroyed."

Jesup called the Indians to a council to give them the bad news. They seemed to know it already, for none showed up. Jesup then staged another of his treacherous performances. On March 21 he sent his troops into the nearby Seminole camp where the Indians had been staying under a truce, safe from harm, they thought. The soldiers disarmed all the warriors and made captive every person they found. The result was the biggest haul of the war: over 500 captives, 150 of them warriors.

By the end of March, the war was almost over for the Seminole blacks. In the previous six months of Jesup's campaign, about 250 blacks had surrendered or been captured. This last move of Jesup's had netted him 167 black captives. Fifteen of them were the runaway slaves of whites, and more than forty were armed warriors. The blacks were hurried off to Tampa Bay and put under strong guard. Except for those reported as "slaves of citizens of Florida." They were delivered to the whites who claimed to be their masters.

The Seminole reds and blacks who had learned to have no faith in Jesup's promises stayed away from Fort Jupiter. Some of the blacks were in bands led by Alligator and John Cavallo, the last black chief still in the field. Jesup sent Abraham and Holatoochee, Cavallo's brother-in-law, to talk to them. Discouraged by the turn of events, both leaders surrendered, Alligator bringing in eighty-eight Indians and Cavallo twenty-seven blacks. When word of this spread, another 360 came in, including a hundred warriors. From now on, blacks played no major part in Seminole resistance. A small number carried on the struggle—as warriors, interpreters, counselors—but there would be no more large engagements in which as many blacks could be counted as reds.

Sick of serving in a war whose end no one could foresee, General Jesup asked to be relieved. He had put in eighteen months as commander. The result: about three thousand Seminole taken out of action. A hundred had been killed, the rest captured. The war was costing the United States almost half a million dollars a month now. In a lament to the Senate, Daniel Webster said, "This Florida war has already cost us over twenty million dollars"—four times the cost of buying Florida from Spain.

On May 15, 1838, Jesup gladly went back to his old duties as quartermaster general of the army.

Now Zachary Taylor had the job of forcing the Indians west.

15

A Stink to the World

"Old Rough-and-Ready" was what they called Zach Taylor, because he shunned fancy dress and was always ready for a fight. His craggy face, easy manner, and superior swearing made him a favorite of the troops. When he took over command from Jesup, he faced the biggest job the army had yet given him. Up to this time he had operated only on small stretches of the frontier. Now he had to find a way to finish up a war.

Under War Department order to curb expenses, he disbanded most of the Florida militia units in the service. Then he picked up the plan General Scott had tried. He divided the territory containing hostile Seminole into twenty-mile-square sectors and assigned a garrison of twenty regulars to each. The troops busied themselves opening posts and building wagon roads to move military supplies. But there was little fighting as a year passed. The Seminole ducked the troops while carrying out sporadic raids for supplies and horses.

Taylor is still another failure as a general, the Florida

whites said. Reducing the militia has only made it easier for the Indians to raid. Behind their charge was the desire to get back on the federal payroll and to resume the profiteering that came from supplying the troops. Nor did they like the way General Taylor handled the question of the blacks. To many of the local citizenry, the Florida war was a convenient means to cash in on captured blacks. When Washington tried to cut the cost of the war, Florida politicians suggested that the fighting be financed by the sale of captured blacks.

Such thinking was opposed by General Taylor. Though a slaveholder himself, he tried to make the Indians and the blacks understand that his army was not engaged in a slave hunt. Nor did he shift his position from day to day the way Jesup had. He told Secretary Poinsett that he would not help separate the Seminole from their blacks, nor would he reduce to slavery any blacks who had lived in freedom.

His position, of course, ran counter to what the government maintained was its obligation to return any slave to his legal owner. But Taylor found a way to get around that.

There were still small bands of Seminole living on the Apalachicola River, and blacks among them. Many of these Seminole had stayed out of the war or sided with the whites. (It did not save them from being forced to migrate, however.) In October 1838, Taylor appeared with a small force and got them all to agree to move west. The general had his first chance to prove his policy. He did not set himself up as a judge of their complexion or their pedigree. And he refused to let any white planters come in to inspect these people or to interfere with his disposal of them. Under the general name of "Apalachees," 220, including blacks, were quietly shipped to the West for resettlement.

Theirs was a much smoother migration than one that had begun that summer of 1838. The trouble centered on the seventy blacks captured by the Creek troops. Promised $8,000 by General Jesup for their slave plunder, the Creeks had rejected the offer and sold their captives to a James Watson of Georgia for $15,000. The blacks were now among the hundreds of Seminole in New Orleans awaiting shipment up the Mississippi to Indian Territory.

Watson sent his brother-in-law, Nathaniel Collins, to find and claim his slaves. He was backed by Secretary Poinsett's authority, but the army officers at the port refused to hand over the blacks. Collins sued, and General Gaines, now in command at New Orleans, came into court and testified that all the blacks held were prisoners of war. They could not be given up to anyone. I will not do what this "voracious claimant" desires, he said. It is "repugnant to law, unjust and iniquitous." These blacks, he told the court, were never captured from whites "in the present, or in any former war."

But the judge ruled against the general. Under the laws of Louisiana, these people, being black, were presumed to be slaves to some person. So why not to the claimant? There seemed to be no hope now for the blacks. For over a century, helped by the government, they had defied the efforts of slaveholders to enchain them. Now everything was lost.

But before Collins could shackle his prizes, Lieutenant John G. Reynolds, the marine officer in charge of the migration, hurried the alleged property aboard ship and sailed up the river toward Arkansas.

The enraged Collins chased them, and caught up at Vicksburg, where they stopped to take on supplies. The Seminole stormed at Collins when he came on board. What right had this slave-catcher to hound them? They were on the edge of mutiny, Reynolds saw, and he was in a difficult position. Collins had the judge's ruling in his hand, and the young marine officer knew well that back in Washington neither the Secretary of War nor the Indian Commissioner wanted the blacks to reach the Western reservation, for they might become an explosive issue between the Seminole and the Creeks.

Collins stayed on board until the expedition reached Little Rock. He prevailed on Reynolds to try to convince the Seminole to let the blacks go peacefully. But the Indians stood so firm that it was plain nothing but force could budge them. Reynolds asked the governor of Arkansas (a slave state) for soldiers to seize the blacks, but was turned down. The governor did not want to have Indians "irritated to madness" turned loose on his frontier lest there be a massacre of whites. No, on the contrary, he would guarantee the Seminole that the blacks would not be taken from them.

Reynolds was relieved to hear that. He moved on to Fort Gibson, where again he dutifully asked General Arbuckle, army commander in the Western country, to supply the force needed to carry out his orders. No, thanks, Arbuckle said. He would have no part of it.

And so the blacks did reach the Indian Territory together with the Seminole. All told, in this first party there were three to four hundred blacks and nine hundred Indians who had been made to move west by one means or another.

Before the year was out, some two thousand Seminole were taken west. Many who had known terrible hardships in the war continued to suffer, although it was now over for them. They were kept waiting for weeks or months in stinking concentration camps in Tampa, Mobile, New Orleans. Weakened by imprisonment, they were crowded on ships and fed badly along the way. (Fifty-four died on the Reynolds trip alone.) And always there was the need to fight off claims of slave dealers for the blacks. Those who survived often found that the promised clothing, tools, and transport were not waiting for them in the West.

Many military officers, like Lieutenant Reynolds, felt sympathy for the Seminole. Some thought there was no need to remove the Indians and that the way it was done was inhumane. "The government is in the wrong," wrote Major Ethan Allen Hitchcock in his diary, "and this is the chief cause of the persevering opposition of the Indians, who have nobly defended their country against our attempt to enforce a fraudulent treaty." The

Seminole's sin, wrote Lieutenant John T. Sprague, "is patriotism, as true as ever burned in the heart of the most civilized."

The same feelings were spreading through the North and even to many in the South. In the spring of 1838, public attention was focused on the removal of seventeen thousand Cherokees, scheduled to begin late in May. The injustice of it roused the great Concord writer Ralph Waldo Emerson to speak out. On April 23 he sent an open letter to President Van Buren which, because of its author's standing, was given wide dissemination.

Emerson spoke of the "sinister rumors" that the President, the Cabinet, and the Congress had agreed to put the whole Cherokee nation into carts and boats and drag them over mountains and rivers to a wilderness far beyond the Mississippi. He wrote:

> In the name of God, sir, we ask you if this be so. . . . Men and women with pale and perplexed faces meet one another in the streets and churches here, and ask if this be so. . . . The piety, the principle that is left in the United States . . . forbid us to entertain it as a fact. Such a dereliction of all faith and virtue, such a denial of justice, and such a deafness to screams for mercy were never heard of in times of peace and in the dealing of a nation with its own allies and wards, since the earth was made.
>
> Sir, does this government think that the people of

the United States are become savage and mad? From their mind are the sentiments of love and a good nature wiped clean out? The soul of man, the justice, the mercy that is the heart's heart in all men, from Maine to Georgia, does abhor this business. . . .

A crime is projected that confounds our understanding by its magnitude, a crime that really deprives us as well as the Cherokees of a country for how could we call the conspiracy that should crush these poor Indians our government, or the land that was cursed by their parting and dying imprecations our country any more?

You, sir, will bring down that renowned chair in which you sit into infamy if your seal is set to this instrument of perfidy; and the name of this nation, hitherto the sweet omen of religion and liberty, will stink to the world. . . .

Emerson went on to urge the President to look behind the Indian-removal policy to see what it revealed of the character of the government. A great many people, he wrote, have already lost all hope that any good will come of appealing to the government to desist from such an act of fraud and robbery as Indian removal. They were gloomy and despondent about the moral character of the government. He asked the President:

Will the American government steal? Will it lie? Will it kill? . . . Our counsellors and old statesmen here say that ten years ago they would have staked their lives on the affirmation that the proposed Indian measures would not be executed; that the unanimous country would put them down. And now the steps of this crime follow each other so fast, at such fatally quick time, that the millions of virtuous citizens, whose agents the government are, have no place to interpose, and must shut their eyes until the last howl and wailing of these tormented villagers and tribes shall afflict the ear of the world.

But the President had already ordered General Scott—the same Scott who was the first to try to remove the Seminole—to march into Cherokee country and use whatever force was needed to compel that people's removal. Mr. Emerson's letter did not change Van Buren's mind.

What Emerson was saying began to reach the floor of Congress through petitions to halt the Cherokee removal. Southerners were quick to try to gag the protest. Calling the Indians "lazy, thieving and murderous savages," Congressman Turney of Tennessee said their defenders were "nothing more or less than a branch of Abolitionism in disguise." The petitioners, he went on, are "the same set of people who, under the false and pretended garb of religion, were straining every nerve for the nefarious purpose of exciting the slaves of the South to insurrection and bloodshed. Why all this apparent sympathy in behalf of the Indians? Is it because they murder the women and children on our Southern frontier? Or is it because they think that they would be important allies to the slaves in the event of their rebellion against the whites? Or is it because they desire to reward the Cherokees for their treachery in Florida, when they went there under the pretence of friendship, and for the laudable purpose of advising the Seminoles to peace, but secretly advising them to fight on. . . ."

While debaters tried to score points in Congress, in Florida the Seminole went on struggling to stay where they were. One week a dozen Indians might be captured and another week a dozen whites killed. The Floridians demanded that Washington do something to stop the raids. In March 1839, Secretary Poinsett ordered the top-ranking general, Alexander Macomb, to go to Florida and calm things down. He was given leeway to do anything he thought would end the war.

In a talk with Taylor, Macomb learned that the general on the scene now believed the Indians could be pacified only if they were allowed to stay in Florida. It was several weeks before Macomb could get any Indians to meet with him. On May 18, two chiefs—Chitto Tustenuggee and Halleck Tustenuggee—came in to Fort King for a parley. Macomb, outdoing the splendor displayed by General Scott, paraded his dragoons in full dress as his band played rousing march tunes. The Indians sat silent, puffing on their pipes. After two days in council, Macomb and the Indians reached an oral agreement. Within two months the Indians would withdraw south of Pease Creek to an area roughly comprising the southwestern quarter of Florida. There they would stay in peace "until further agreements could be reached." Meanwhile, the United States would cease all military action.

It is not clear how permanent or how temporary the Seminole considered the agreement to be. But Macomb must have been satisfied, because he proclaimed that the war was over and he returned to Washington. Neither the commanding general nor the government had taken into account public opinion in Florida and the fact that only two chiefs had come to the Fort King sessions. At least three bands of hostile Seminole operating in this region had not been represented. One was led by Hospetarke, and another by Otalke Thlocco. Chakaika headed a third group consisting of Spanish Indians who had taken no part in the war till now, probably because they lived so far from the main battlegrounds.

Although these bands avoided action against the army, they harried the "cracker" whites who had always shown such contempt for them. General Taylor believed the whites even provoked the Indians, in order to keep federal funds pouring into the peninsula.

News of the Fort King agreement infuriated white Florida. The Tallahassee *Floridian* cried "Shame! Shame! Shame!" and insisted that whites shoot Indians on sight in revenge for old wrongs. The St. Augustine *News* charged that the government had stooped to begging for peace and urged the citizens to a united protest. A mass meeting in Tallahassee resolved that no Indians should be allowed to remain in Florida: they could be expected to join any foreign foe who landed on the coast to attack the United States. And besides, they would never cease giving refuge to runaway slaves.

If the Seminole who took part in the Fort King parley believed theirs was a permanent agreement, they soon learned otherwise. On June 22 a letter from Secretary Poinsett was published in the press stating: "I am of the opinion that the arrangement made by General Macomb will . . . enable me to remove the Indians from the territory much sooner than can be done by force."

These words appeased the Floridians but enraged the Seminole. Once more the government was saying removal was inevitable. As though in response, Indians attacked and killed a white family near Tallahassee and then ambushed an army wagon train in central Florida. Their next move smashed the shaky peace agreement.

It happened on the Caloosahatchee. As part of the Fort King agreement, Taylor had set up a trading post on the river within the bounds of the Indian reservation. A trader was sent in to handle the business, and to protect the post Taylor assigned twenty-six soldiers under Lieutenant Colonel William S. Harney, a strapping dragoon famed as a tough Indian fighter.

One night in July, Harney came back from a boar hunt and, taking off his clothes, lay down in his tent to sleep. Rifle shots woke him at dawn. (It turned out that no guard had been posted.) Rushing out of his tent wearing only his drawers, the colonel found the camp under surprise assault from a force of about 160 Seminole, divided into two bands. One, led by Hospetarke, was looting the trader's store. The other, led by Chakaika, was attacking the troops. The confused soldiers fled to the river but could not escape over it because Indians were firing from both banks. Harney sprinted for the river, where he saw that his men were unarmed. An officer had forgotten to pass out ammunition for the new Colt rifles, and the soldiers, discovering their guns were empty, had flung them away. Knowing defense was hopeless, Harney ran downstream beyond the lines of Indians and found a canoe to escape in.

Thirteen soldiers and three civilians were killed. The Indians took some $3,000 in trade goods and $1,500 in silver coins, besides the Colt rifles.

The massacre of the soldiers and traders ended any hope of a truce. The whites charged the Seminole with treachery for betraying Macomb's agreement. But the bands who attacked Harney's force had never ratified it. The Seminole who did agree to it could not speak for Hospetarke or Chakaika.

Within days of the disaster, the fighting was on again, ever more bitter and bloody on both sides. When Taylor's men rounded up about two hundred prisoners, the general said he would free them if the killers of Harney's men were surrendered to him. Governor Call cried for Taylor to quit and asked that he himself be given command again. Call's interference only brought about his own removal as governor by Secretary Poinsett, who acted with President Van Buren's support.

Call retaliated by charging publicly that Poinsett was "responsible to his country for the blood which has been shed through the weakness and imbecility of his administration of the War Department."

With Call ousted, Robert Reid assumed the governorship. He was considered a "gentleman," an "intellectual," and a "humanitarian," but he sounded like the man he succeeded. This war, he declared, is waged against "beasts of prey." It was only fitting, then, that the governor and his legislative council call for the use of bloodhounds against these "fiends in human shape."

The Floridians knew that on the island of Jamaica the whites had used Cuban bloodhounds against the rebellious slaves. The Maroon Revolt had gone on for eighty years and was ended only when the bloodhounds were brought in to track down the revolutionaries in their mountain hideouts.

The American army welcomed the proposal that the same be done here. It felt the dogs would protect its troops from surprise and ambush, and could help track the Indians to their hiding places in the swamps and hammocks. So thirty-three bloodhounds were bought in Cuba, at $151.72 each—a fantastic price—and four handlers were imported with them. As soon as news of their arrival appeared in the Northern press, protests began to mount. Quakers petitioned Congress against so inhuman a weapon. Senator Daniel Webster sought assurances from the government that the hounds would not be let loose. Former President John Quincy Adams, now a congressman, ridiculed the War Department. He asked the House to direct Secretary Poinsett to report on "the natural, political and martial history of the bloodhounds, showing the peculiar fitness of that class of warriors to be the associates of the gallant army of the United States, specifying the nice discrimination of his scent between the blood of the freeman and the blood of the slave, between the blood of savage Seminoles and that of the Anglo-Saxon pious Christian. . . . Also, whether he deems it expedient to extend to the said bloodhounds and their posterity the benefits of the pension laws. . . ."

Refusing to let the army outdistance it in the use of such modern weapons, the navy and the marines imported bloodhounds too. Army experiments with the dogs were at first reported to be a great success. When the dogs helped capture some Indians, the Jacksonville *Advocate* coined the term "peace hounds" for them.

But Poinsett was nervous over the criticism. He instructed General Taylor to confine the hounds to tracking, and to keep them leashed and muzzled. They were not to "disturb" Indian women or children, either.

More trials of the dogs took place under combat conditions. Florida's swamps and waterways made it impossible for the dogs to follow the trail of a Seminole for any significant distance. When the navy tried out the hounds, their luck was no better. The dogs failed to find any Seminole and one of the hounds dropped dead of exhaustion. A story spread that the Seminole had cleverly learned how to make friends with the dogs, which rendered the whole experiment useless. Whatever the reason, the dogs were a failure. They moved the war no closer to its end and brought the government only ridicule and contempt.

Wood engraving from an 1836 pamphlet written by Captain James Barr, a Louisiana volunteer in the Second Seminole War. The white author stresses the "barbarity" of the Indians and the blacks. COURTESY OF MILTON MELTZER

Winfield Scott, the first general sent in to remove the Seminole. His orders were to fight until the last fugitive slave was taken from the Seminole, and to force an unconditional surrender upon the Indians. THE NEW YORK PUBLIC LIBRARY PICTURE COLLECTION

Zachary Taylor, who directed the biggest battle of the Seminole War, at Lake Okeechobee. Although a slaveholder himself, he opposed the government policy of assigning the army to a slave hunt. THE NEW YORK PUBLIC LIBRARY PICTURE COLLECTION

George Catlin, the American artist, spent most of his life studying and painting the Indians. This pencil drawing is one of many portraits he made of the Seminole in 1838, when Osceola and others were held prisoner at Fort Moultrie in South Carolina. Standing with gun at left is Yaholocoochee, a chief. Next to him, with pipe, is King Philip. At right is the twelve-year-old nephew of Osceola. Sitting, from left, is Coa Hadjo, a chief; La-Shee, a warrior; and Wont-Now, a warrior's wife, with her child.
COURTESY OF THE NEW YORK HISTORICAL SOCIETY, NEW YORK CITY

In May 1837, during an armistice in the Seminole War, Captain John R. Vinton, U.S. Army, made this pencil drawing of Osceola at Lake Monroe, Florida. Depicted more often than any other Seminole leader, Osceola became a legendary figure in his own short lifetime. The accuracy of the likeness is attested to by General Hernandez, who on General Jesup's orders violated a flag of truce to seize Osceola at Camp Peyton in October 1837. COURTESY OF MUSEUM OF THE AMERICAN INDIAN, HEYE FOUNDATION

For twenty-two years Joshua R. Giddings of Ohio fought in the House of Representatives in defense of Indians and for black liberation. This is the title page of his book about the Seminole War. James Russell Lowell urged every American to read it as an "indictment which recites crimes which have been committed in his name, perpetrated by troops and officials in his service, and all done at his expense. The whole nation is responsible at the bar of the world for these atrocities, devised by members of its Cabinets and its Congress, directed by its Presidents, and executed by its armies and its courts." AMERICAN HISTORY DIVISION, THE NEW YORK PUBLIC LIBRARY, ASTOR, LENOX AND TILDEN FOUNDATIONS

This lithograph of Tuchose Emathla, called John Hicks by the whites, was made after an oil painting by C. B. King, illustrator of the McKenney and Hall study, *The Indian Tribes of North America* (1838–42). The Seminole leader was elected Supreme Chief of all the Florida Indians in 1826. He was one of the seven chiefs on the delegation sent to Arkansas in 1832–33 to study the Western territory offered the Seminole if they would quit Florida. SMITHSONIAN INSTITUTION, NATIONAL ANTHROPOLOGICAL ARCHIVES

Abraham, a Florida slave in his youth, became one of the most influential blacks to serve with the Seminole as interpreter and counselor. He resisted the federal removal policy because he knew it would be fatal to his people. AMERICAN HISTORY DIVISION, THE NEW YORK PUBLIC LIBRARY, ASTOR, LENOX AND TILDEN FOUNDATIONS

Coacoochee (called Wildcat) was one of the most militant and eloquent Seminole leaders. He made a sensational escape from army captivity but years later was imprisoned a second time and shipped to the West. AMERICAN HISTORY DIVISION, THE NEW YORK PUBLIC LIBRARY, ASTOR, LENOX AND TILDEN FOUNDATIONS

This portrait of Osceola was painted by George Catlin at Fort Moultrie in South Carolina, shortly before the captive Seminole leader died in 1838. Catlin described him as an "extraordinary character . . . the master spirit and leader of the tribe," now "grieving with a broken spirit, and ready to die, cursing white man, no doubt, to the end of his breath." COURTESY OF THE NATIONAL COLLECTION OF FINE ARTS, SMITHSONIAN INSTITUTION

16

The Turning Point

Now the army was bigger than ever, thanks to the Seminole War, but it was doing no better. A sense of futility had settled over the men assigned to the Florida front. This had become a war without battles. A handful of soldiers might run into a small party of Seminole and a flurry of shots would be exchanged. Rarely did troops encounter more than ten warriors. Such actions could not be dignified as skirmishes, much less battles. Scouts would slip into swamps and return to report nothing but the killing of a snake. Crocodiles they might see, but no Seminole.

Boredom lay as thick over the troops as the suffocating heat of summer. Insects stung the body, sands burned the skin, the saw grass cut the feet and legs. When the weather turned wet, mud and water made the earth a quagmire. Captain Nathaniel Hunter, a young West Pointer, commanding a fortified post in the southern part of the peninsula, wrote in his diary:

> Rain, rain, rain, will it never cease its eternal patter? What a melancholy sound that monotonous pat, pat, pat as it falls from the eaves or trickles through the crevices of the roof just where your head happens to be. If such a reminder were to happen in London, half of it would be depopulated by suicide. Men and horses are performing the most arduous service and exposed to all the inclemencies of this variable climate. I presume the General will leave this God-abandoned country at an early date. I would urge it most strenuously.

In March 1840, Hunter's men were coming down with malaria and yellow fever faster than he could get them to the hospital. Assigned to another post, he found its filth unbelievable: "What mountains of manure. What stenches, stinks and odours that emanate therefrom." Then Hunter himself fell sick and after five months of illness felt broken in spirit and hopeless.

Desertion in his command was common now. Soldiers shot or amputated themselves to escape duty. Useless paper work was drowning the officers. And for what? Hunter asked himself. Why am I in Florida? He began to wonder about the morality of a government that used the army to force Indians out of their homeland.

In April, when he received General Taylor's order to take no more Indians alive, Hunter confided to his diary that he would not obey the order. He could not live with himself if he consented to such an act of murder. No, he would not let any Seminole prisoner taken in his command be executed. In his diary he wrote, "I've tried every argument to still my conscience." To the questions his conscience raised, he set down the standard answers: "That I have no right to discuss the propriety of my order; that it is the duty of a soldier to obey; that government is but enforcing a treaty; that our enemies are barbarous murderers of women and children; and last, that I am paid for acting not thinking. . . ."

Then he challenged himself: "Have God and justice no claim upon you prior and paramount to the commission of a crime? Will no compunctions deter you from wringing your hands in innocent blood, even though it be the command of a superior officer? Enforce a treaty, a compact begot in fraud and brought forth in the blackest villainy?"

General Taylor, too, had had his fill of this war. In April 1840 he resigned command, and the next month Brevet Brigadier General Walker Keith Armistead took over. Now fifty-five, Armistead was a West Pointer and also a veteran of the War of 1812. He had already tasted Florida service twice, under Jesup's command.

The new commander divided the peninsula into an upper and a lower zone. He turned over defense of the northern sector, above Fort King, to Florida's militia, and gave his regulars the job of driving out the Seminole below the line. Most of the Indians had gone deeper and deeper south, where they would have been happy to cultivate a patch of ground in peace. But the troops had their orders to kill or capture the enemy and the Indians had constantly to be on the move.

Only two bands of Seminole, led by Coacoochee and Halleck Tustenuggee, stayed around the upper settlements. In mid-May, Coacoochee with about one hundred warriors attacked an army detachment and killed six men. Then he ambushed two wagons coming out of St. Augustine, killing five men. One of the wagons contained eighteen trunks of theatrical costumes belonging to a troupe of touring actors.

Trying guerrilla tactics, the army began to make some progress against the Indians. Special units managed to find and destroy cultivated fields which the Indians had kept secret for years, as well as a hidden coastal village where the Seminole had carried on trade with ships from the Caribbean islands.

Constant scouting and partisan action gave Armistead hope that, with a little bribery, he could finish up the war. The government gave him a fund of some $50,000 for this purpose. In November he got Thlocko Tustenuggee and Halleck Tustenuggee, two of the leading chiefs who were still resisting, to meet him at Fort King. The general offered them $5,000 each to surrender with their bands. They asked to stay two weeks to think it over, fed and supplied themselves at the army's expense meanwhile, then silently disappeared again. But here and there Armistead found a chief who accepted the money and gave up. Coosa Tustenuggee, a Mikasuki, took $5,000 for bringing in his band of sixty. Lesser chiefs settled for $200, and warriors got $30 and a rifle.

Now Washington decided on a new device: to get Seminole who had gone west to return and persuade those still in Florida to emigrate too. Twelve Indians came back in a delegation, but what they had to say to their brethren had the opposite effect from what the government intended. Captain John T. Sprague, who was there, explained why:

> Had the enemy been kept totally ignorant of the country allotted them, better results might have been anticipated; but what they had gathered from the honest confessions and silence of their brothers, tended to make them venerate, with more fidelity and increased love, the soil which they had defended, with heroic fortitude, for five consecutive years.

The delegation said the government had not kept its promise to give them a territory for their separate use. They were without home or country now, living on Cherokee lands, under Cherokee protection to prevent the nearby Creeks from enslaving the Seminole blacks. Game was scarce in this cold and dreary land, and many of their people had sickened and died. This report led some of the Indians who were awaiting deportation to escape back into the swamps.

With the Western delegation gone, Lieutenant Colonel Harney set out on a Seminole hunt. It was eighteen months since his troops had been massacred on the Caloosahatchee and he had fled for his life. In December he led a canoeing expedition of ninety men into the Everglades. They were guided by a black prisoner named John, who may have chosen to betray the Seminole in exchange for his freedom. Moving from island to island, they captured some Seminole, whom Harney ordered to be hanged on the spot. When they drew near the island John said was Chakaika's headquarters, Harney paused to dress and paint his men like Indians. Soon after sunrise, the disguised troops beached their canoes and surprised Chakaika as he was chopping wood alone. A soldier shot him dead. The troops attacked the Indian camp and wiped out the band, taking only three warriors prisoner. Harney hanged two of these, and next to them the corpse of Chakaika. He let one man live, to use him as a guide.

News of the hangings infuriated the Indians, but the Florida legislative council commended Harney and presented him with a fancy sword. Later that month, the Indians attacked a party of thirteen soldiers escorting an officer's wife from one post to another. They killed the woman and four men. The settlements around St. Augustine panicked at the thought that there were still Indians able to raid so close to their homes.

But slowly Armistead continued to round up Indians for removal. By February 1841 there were 270 at Tampa awaiting shipment west. In March the general thought he had the biggest catch of all. Coacoochee, dressed in one of the splendid Shakespearean costumes he had captured in his raid on the wagon train, came in for a talk. The officers recognized him as Hamlet, and next to him warriors garbed as Horatio and Richard III.

As the talks were about to begin, Coacoochee's little daughter, whom he had thought killed but whom the whites had captured, came to him. In her hands she offered her father the bullets and powder she had secretly collected against the time he would come for her. The chief wept openly before the council.

Captain Sprague, observing him, wrote that when his time came to talk, Coacoochee's "youth, his manly bearing, his intelligent face, the calm subdued intonations of his voice, his fluent speech and graceful gestures, won the sympathy of those around, and commanded the respect and attention of all."

The Seminole leader related what had been done to the Indians since the war had begun. Then he said:

> The whites dealt unjustly by me. I came to them, they deceived me. The land I was upon I loved, my body is made of its sands; the Great Spirit gave me legs to walk over it, hands to aid myself, eyes to see its ponds, rivers, forests, and game, then a head with which I think. The sun, which is warm and bright as my feelings are now, shines to warm us and bring forth our crops, and the moon brings back the spirits of our warriors, our fathers, wives, and children. The white man comes; he

grows pale and sick. Why cannot we live here in peace? I have said that I am the enemy to the white man. I could live in peace with him, but they first steal our cattle and horses, cheat us, and take our lands. The white men are as thick as the leaves in the hammock; they come upon us thicker every year. They may shoot us, drive our women and children night and day; they may chain our hands and feet, but the red man's heart will be always free.

There were more such meetings with Coacoochee in the following months, the army being patient because his influence could be great if he chose to persuade his people to emigrate. Sprague said the chief "admitted the necessity of his leaving the country, hard as it was"—but cautioned it would not be easy to get others to agree.

At the end of May, Armistead asked to be relieved. In the year of his command he had shipped 450 reds and blacks west and had another 236 at the port waiting to go. He said 120 of those already gone were warriors. He believed there could be no more than 300 warriors still in Florida.

The War Department accepted Armistead's request, and gave the command to Colonel William Jenkins Worth. Worth, the son of Quakers, had been lamed by a bullet in the War of 1812. He had served as commandant of West Point for eight years and recently as head of the new Eighth Infantry in Florida. A strong man who looked handsome on a horse, he displayed great confidence in combat. He was rated a capable but painfully vain officer.

Worth's job was not made easier by the turn in public opinion. The war was becoming ever more unpopular. The very words—"The Florida War"—disgusted Congress. The effect, however, was to make the legislators hand out money freely for any scheme that promised to bring "this damn war" to an end.

Early in 1841 Congress was asked for more money, this time so that the army could pay the Seminole to give themselves up. This triggered another debate. Giddings, the Ohio abolitionist, asked for the floor. The House knew he had prepared a speech whose purpose was to prove that the true aim of the war was to help slaveholders recover fugitives from their plantations.

The Southerners had all along tried to prevent discussion of this subject. Since 1836 they had successfully invoked the gag rule which tabled all anti-slavery petitions and throttled debate on the issue. Now they insisted that the gag rule did not permit Giddings to say what they knew he wanted to say. But the congressman from Maine who was presiding decided it was appropriate to examine the causes of the war.

Giddings poured out fact after fact about the war, all taken from public documents, and charged that the United States had no right to engage in such a war or to tax the people for its maintenance. "This war is therefore unconstitutional, unjust, and an outrage upon the rights of the people of the free states," he said.

Mr. Cooper of Georgia rose in a fury: "We of the South have a different and more exalted patriotism—one which is neither measured by our purse, our love of Indians and Negroes, nor our love of money. No, sir. Though you were at war for a petty strip of land on your Northeastern boundary, fit only for firewood, Southern products, Southern money, and Southern blood would be at your command. We should not stop to inquire whether your war was *just or unjust*. . . . We should hold it to be our country's cause; and for her cause and her honor we would bleed and die."

Defending the army's use of bloodhounds, and Harney's hanging of the captured Indians, Cooper went on to say that "the most reasonable complaint would be that those who waged the war did not make it a war of extermination from the beginning. In the end that policy would have proved a saving of much human life, and millions of money."

Another Georgian, Mr. Black, made heated answer to Giddings. How dare the Ohioan make an abolition speech about a bill to provide money to remove the Indians? But then Mr. Black himself would not vote for the bill—for reasons quite different from Giddings's. "I will vote for no $100,000 to buy up our peace from the Seminole warriors," he said. "If the money is wanted to redouble your forces—if I could be assured it would be expended in exterminating these savage hell-hounds from that ill-fated land, and in offering them up as a sacrifice to appease the blood which cries aloud from every hearthstone in Florida, I would freely and joyfully give it. But I would sooner see the whole Territory abandoned by its inhabitants and sunk in the Atlantic ocean, than vote one dollar to propitiate those whom we ought to conquer."

He assured the House that if Giddings had the courage to come to Georgia, he would be lynched.

When the debate ended, Congress voted in favor of the appropriation bill. A month later, it authorized the expenditure of another million dollars for the war.

But the discussion initiated by Giddings was published and widely circulated among the people. It helped educate them to the true nature of the Seminole War and gave new life to the abolition cause. More, it made Southerners realize that there was little point in keeping the gag rule in force if, under it, a speech like Giddings' could be made. The rule was repealed in the next Congress.

In the summer of 1841 Worth tried a new means of conquering the Seminole. Arms had failed to defeat them, and all the offers made at peace talks had failed to break their resistance. He would try to grind them down by relentlessly destroying their crops, their shelters, and their sources of supply. What his army did was summed up neatly by Lieutenant Sprague: "Tracks seen, fields destroyed, country waded, troops exhausted, Indians gone."

It was almost impossible for Worth to come to grips with the Indians, however. They continued to avoid all encounters. They knew they could leave it to the climate to fight their battles. It had long ago proved more destructive to the troops than the rifle or the scalping knife. The only way to defeat the Indians, it seemed, was to blanket the peninsula with troops so that the enemy could no longer hunt or fish.

Worth did not have the manpower for that, but he encouraged a partisan kind of warfare. He sought out young and ambitious officers and offered them no restraints. Their order was: "Find the enemy, capture or exterminate."

On June 15, Coacoochee was seized, with fifteen of his warriors. He was visiting Fort Pierce on a peace parley when a junior officer decided to make him prisoner. The chief was brought to Tampa in shackles to see Colonel Worth. The war was at a turning point now. Lieutenant Sprague, taking part as a member of Colonel Worth's staff, reported the climactic meeting aboard ship. It was the Fourth of July, 1841:

> Coacoochee and his warriors came up slowly to the quarterdeck of the transport, their feet-irons hardly enabling them to step four inches, and arranged themselves according to rank. As they laid their manacled hands upon their knees before them, in the presence of so many whom they had so long hunted as foes, they hung their heads in silence. Not a cheering voice or expression could be seen or heard among the group.

The chief seemed to be waiting for his doom. The colonel arose and, taking Coacoochee by the hand, said:

Coacoochee, I take you by the hand as a warrior, a brave man; you have fought long and with a true and strong heart for your country. I take your hand with feelings of pride; you love your country as we do, it is sacred to you, the ashes of your kindred are dear to you and to the Seminole; these feelings have caused much bloodshed, distress, horrid murders; it is time now the Indian felt the power and strength of the white man. Like the oak, you may bear up for many years against strong winds; the time must come when it will fall; this time has arrived. You have withstood the blasts of five winters, and the storms of thunder, lightning and wind, five summers; the branches have fallen, and the tree, burnt at the roots, is prostrated.

Coacoochee, I am your friend; so is your great father at Washington. What I say to you is true, my tongue is not forked like a snake, my word is for the happiness of the red man. You are a great warrior, the Indians throughout the country look to you as a leader, by your councils they have been governed. This war has lasted five years, much blood has been shed, much innocent blood; you have made your hands, the ground red with the blood of women and children. This war must now end. You are the man to do it; you must and shall accomplish it. I sent for you, that through the exertions of yourself and men, you might induce your entire band to emigrate.

I wish you to state how many days it will require to effect an interview with the Indians in the woods. You can select three or five of these men to carry your talk; name the time, it shall be granted; but I tell you, as I wish your relatives and friends told, that unless they fulfill your demands, yourself, and these warriors now seated before us, shall be hung to the yards of this vessel, when the sun sets on the day appointed, with the irons upon your hands and feet. I tell you this, that we may well understand each other. I do not wish to frighten you, you are too brave a man for that; but I say what I mean, and I will do it. It is for the benefit of the white and red man. This war must end, and you must end it.

There was a long silence, broken only by the grating noise of shackles as a warrior shifted position. Then Coacoochee stood up to answer Colonel Worth:

I was once a boy, then I saw the white man afar off. I hunted in the woods, first with a bow and arrow, then with a rifle. I saw the white man, and was told he was my enemy. I could not shoot him as I would a wolf or a bear; yet like these he came upon me; horses, cattle, and fields, he took from me. He said he was my friend; he abused our women and children, and told us to go from the land. Still he gave me his hand in friendship; we took it; whilst taking it, he had a snake in the other, his tongue was forked; he lied, and stung us. I asked but for a small piece of these lands, enough to plant and to live

> upon far south, a spot where I could place the ashes of my kindred, a spot only sufficient upon which I could lay my wife and child. This was not granted me. I was put in prison; I escaped. I have been again taken; you have brought me back; I am here; I feel the irons in my heart. . . .
>
> It is true I have fought like a man, so have my warriors; but the whites are too strong for us. I wish now to have my band around me and go to Arkansas. . . . I never wish to tread upon my land unless I am free.

Worth held Coacoochee in prison while five of his warriors were freed to carry the message of migration to their people. They had forty days in which to do it, or their chief would be hanged.

The Seminole leaders who still refused to yield feared the effect of an appeal from a warrior of Coacoochee's standing. Halleck Tustenuggee, Thlocko Tustenuggee, and other chiefs met with 120 warriors and pledged to kill any messenger—red, black, or white—who came preaching migration.

Worth did not sit by, waiting for the forty days to pass. He sent out small detachments to drive the remaining Seminole from the field. At the same time, he encouraged white settlers to return to their farms, with the promise that the army would protect them. Before five weeks were up, Coacoochee's messengers rounded up all his band but twenty, enough to appease Worth. From this time on, Coacoochee cooperated with the army. Worth let the chief go out into the back country on his own, to spread the word that the Seminole should go west. Soon Hospetarke, now almost eighty-five, came in with fifteen men, and by the fall another three hundred of the old chief's followers had given up. In October, Worth shipped Coacoochee and Hospetarke west. With them were almost three hundred Seminole, eighteen of them blacks.

A kind of truce had been kept in the upper zone, but the Indians still at large in the south continued to fight. To capture them, Worth sent out joint army-navy expeditions. The abandoned camps and fields they found told them the Seminole had split up into small groups of four or five for safety. The Indians moved by night, wiping out every trace of their footprints. They jumped from log to log in the swamps or hammocks, walked backward or crept on hands and knees, crossed and recrossed their tracks. One officer said it "was like hunting a wolf, who at night would look into your camp, and follow your footsteps at noonday."

But, despite great losses due to illness, the soldiers pursued the Seminole in all seasons. They destroyed dozens of cultivated fields, five to twenty acres in extent, and burned down hundreds of sheds and huts. The Indians were driven from hiding place to hiding place. Their crops ruined, they were scarcely able to exist, because fear of exposing their position by rifleshot deprived them of game, too.

In October another delegation of Seminole chiefs, headed by Alligator, came from the West to try to coax the last intransigents to give up. Alligator persuaded Thlocko Tustenuggee and his brother to come in, bringing 162 people with them. All through the winter months the troops chased after Halleck Tustenuggee, who kept harassing the Floridians, killing, burning, and taking loot. More than once the army thought it had the chief's band surrounded, only to find that he had slipped through.

Nevertheless, Worth managed to thin out the resistance. Early in February 1842, he shipped another 230 Seminole west, 68 of them warriors. That left 301 still at large, he estimated—112 of them warriors. Because they were so few, he did not think it practicable to round them up in the swamps by force. It is time to cut down military strength in Florida, he told Washington, and deploy the forces that remain so that they can protect the white settlements. Let me tell the three hundred Seminole they may stay where they are and start their farming again, so long as they are peaceable. If they want to come in to our posts, let us welcome them, and try to persuade them to go west. Let us stop the fighting now. Can it be good public policy, he asked, "to prosecute the contest for results so uncertain, at expense so enormous"?

Washington turned down Worth's proposal. Of all the high officers who discussed it in council, only General Jesup supported Worth. It was as though the top men—civilian and military alike—felt the honor of the nation and the gallantry of the army would be stained if they let a single Seminole survive in Florida. They had to prove the power of the American army and demonstrate the blessings of a bottomless treasury. So Worth was told to keep hounding the Indians till they all gave up. A bounty of $100 for every warrior captured or killed was offered to the soldiers. Week after week the army hunted through the hammocks, cutting down the Seminole warrior by warrior.

The younger Seminole were the most stubborn fighters. They had grown from boyhood to manhood in the midst of war. They had never known peace, and they looked upon the whites as their natural enemy. Most of the older chiefs were dead or had moved west. The young men followed leaders like Halleck, who had killed his own sister because she wanted to surrender.

A Mikasuki by birth, Halleck was about thirty-five now. He was a lean man, well over six feet tall. His manner in parleys with the whites was modest and unassuming. He smiled as he listened to them, but he never took their advice or followed their example. His independent mind commanded their respect. If they spoke to him as a representative of his people, he promptly said he acted only for himself.

Worth was determined to put Halleck out of action. In April, Indian and black scouts guided the colonel and four hundred of his men to Halleck's hideaway on a hammock near Lake Ahapopka. The forty Seminole warriors were barricaded behind logs, and to get to them the troops had to wade through mud and hack down thick, rotting vegetation whose stink was so terrible that many of the soldiers vomited. From all sides the white firepower poured in so overwhelmingly that the Indians had to abandon their position. They snaked their way into the deep swamp but left most of their gear behind.

It was the last engagement of the war that could be called a battle. Most of Halleck's band escaped, but their leader realized the end was near. Ten days later he came into Worth's camp at Warm Springs to talk under a white flag, bringing two of his wives and two children. The talks dragged on for several days, with Halleck indicating he wished the war would end, but making no promises to emigrate.

Impatient to get it over with, Colonel Worth borrowed General Jesup's familiar tactic of treachery. He invited Halleck to make a visit with him to Fort King. While they were away, the troops gave a feast for Halleck's band at Warm Springs and in the midst of the festivity encircled them with guns and took them prisoner. They crowded the Indians into wagons and rushed them to the embarkation point at Tampa.

A messenger sped to Fort King to tell Worth his coup had succeeded. When Halleck asked what the news was, he learned that all his band were captives and on their way to Tampa. And you yourself, Worth said, are now our prisoner. The betrayal was a dreadful blow. The chief's spirit seemed shattered. "He stood erect," Sprague said, "quivering with excitement, brushing his fingers through his long black hair, his eyes sparkling with fire, his breast heaving in agony, as though about to grasp and tear in pieces the perpetrators in this closing act." The armed guard around him made him realize he could do nothing. He sank to the ground, unconscious.

Worth's double-dealing brought him many prisoners; forty-three warriors, thirty-seven women, and thirty-four children. It was more than a third of the Seminole he had said were still in Florida.

The capture of Halleck's band led the War Department to reconsider Worth's proposal. On May 10, 1842, President John Tyler told Congress that, on "mature reflection," he was satisfied that he could now indulge his "desire to promote the great interests of humanity, and extend the reign of peace and good will, by terminating the unhappy warfare that had so long been carried on. . . ."

The field commander, Colonel Worth, was given the authority to bring this about in any way he saw fit.

Worth went through with his original plan. He offered peace to all the Indians who would remain in an assigned area. But those already in his hands were shipped west. Halleck's band left in July. "I have been hunted like a wolf," the chief said as he boarded ship, "and now I am to be sent away like a dog."

In August, Worth met with those Indian leaders still at large to tell them that every warrior who consented to emigrate would get a rifle, money, and a year's rations. Only a few accepted. The rest chose to settle on the reservation allotted them—essentially the region mapped out for this purpose by General Macomb in 1839.

On August 14, Worth declared the war was over.

He was rewarded by promotion to brigadier general and given a ninety-day leave. As happens so often after an American war, Congress promptly moved to cut the size of the armed forces. Florida objected. While there was even one Indian left in their territory, they wanted action against him.

Their new delegate in Congress, the Democrat David Levy, was a shrewd politician. He charged that President Tyler, leader of the opposition Whig Party, had acted in this manner so as to take the credit for ending an unpopular war. The whites of Florida, he hastened to assert, were not to blame for the war. We merit only praise for our conduct toward the Seminole, he said. But "let us hear no more of sympathy for these Indians. They know no mercy. They are demons, not men. They have the human form, but nothing of the human heart. . . . If they cannot be emigrated, they should be exterminated."

Bloodthirsty words. Florida's whites insisted that the war was not over, not only because hunting and killing Indians was good sport but because it was good business, too. The provisioning of large numbers of troops for costly expeditions into the swamps and hammocks had brought profits to suppliers and work and food to the volunteers. They disliked hearing General Worth say that it was ended. They came to believe this only when the army refused to continue feeding their militia.

17

A Whole People Sentenced

Four thousand Seminole were finally driven into exile by a mighty nation that boasted of its justice, its honor, and its love of liberty. The Florida Indians and blacks defended their homes and their freedom with a desperate tenacity that has few parallels in the annals of colonizers and conquerors. A ragged, starving handful of guerrillas, they defied the power of an invading army ten times their number.

They made America pay a heavy price for its racism —a price we still pay in many ways. What conquering the Indian did to us as a people and a nation we are only beginning to understand. "That process of fraud, corruption, trickery, violence, spread like a sickness through all the American body politic, and those methods are often the methods used still in settling political, social and international problems," wrote Carleton Beals.

For seven years, Administration after Administration carried on a reign of terror in Florida, spending forty million dollars, using the greater part of its armed forces, wasting the lives of fifteen hundred regular troops and an inestimable number of militia and civilians. The suffering of the Indians and blacks through the years of persecution, the lives lost, the property stolen, the friends and families separated—they cannot be measured.

Six eminent generals tried to carry out the national policy of Indian removal; every one of them had to admit that the Seminole were a people who could not be defeated. In the end there were still an indomitable few hundred who refused to give up their homes deep in the swamps.

More than five hundred blacks were seized and enslaved during the war years. Perhaps half of them were born free. The others had escaped from slavery. One of the war's major objectives was this enslavement. The forty million expended from the public treasury was the equivalent of eighty thousand dollars for each black forced into bondage. Put another way, the country paid the lives of three white men for each black enslaved.

Yet the long resistance of the blacks was not in vain. Those attached to the Seminole kept the freedom they or their fathers had won by flight and then defended by arms. If they had not shown a passion for liberty, but let themselves be moved out at the start, they would surely have been made slaves again. As for the slaves who deserted the plantations to join the Seminole at the outbreak of the war, many were killed or captured in the first years. But those who survived won their freedom. The army was forced to classify them as belonging with the Seminole, and they left for the West as free people.

What happened to the Seminole? A year after the war ended, only a little more than three thousand were left in the Indian Territory west of the Mississippi. In 1849, a small disturbance between the whites and the Indians remaining in Florida became known as the Third Seminole War. Another sixty Indians were removed to the West. But for the most part, little was heard of the Indians who stayed in the remote Everglades. Their numbers, so small to begin with, shrank during their isolation and slowly rose again only as the twentieth century set on. By the 1960's there were about a thousand Seminole in Florida, and something more than twice that number in Oklahoma.

By 1850, Indian removal had been accomplished. Only a few small enclaves of Indians were left in the eastern part of the United States that so many Indian nations had occupied before the white man came. The armed power of the federal government had succeeded in ridding the Eastern states of them. No longer did the Indians have any hope of either assimilation or escape. The whites had insisted that they learn new ways or be exterminated. But even when they had adapted themselves to the culture of the invaders, they had been driven from their homes. Their whole way of life was being wiped out. Removed to the West, the Indians had to begin all over again. There they suffered more betrayals, encountered even worse handicaps, and endured still more wars.

It is more than 130 years since the Seminole War ended. And in all that time the federal government has continued its efforts to force the Indians to change their way of life. It is a policy which, as a Senate subcommittee on Indian education reported in 1969, has meant "the destruction and disorganization of Indian communities and individuals," the sentencing of a whole people to "a life of poverty and despair."

Why?

For the same reasons, the senators said, that lay behind the Seminole War: "A continuous desire to exploit and expropriate Indian land and physical resources and a self-righteous intolerance of tribal communities and cultural differences."

When will we learn?

Bibliography

The two scholars to whom I am most deeply indebted are John K. Mahon and Kenneth W. Porter. Professor Mahon's recent *History of the Second Seminole War* is the first and only full-scale study of this important but much neglected episode in American history. Without his pioneering labors, this book would have been infinitely harder to write. Professor Porter's inquiries into the relationship of black Americans—slave and free—to the Seminole, began appearing in the historical journals almost forty years ago, when few other scholars showed any interest in this crucial aspect of Indian removal from Florida. More than a dozen articles by him on many facets of this subject have appeared now. They are an invaluable treasury of useful information and provocative ideas.

Most important among the other sources I drew upon are the *Travels of William Bartram* for that naturalist's superb eyewitness account of early Seminole life, and

Joshua R. Giddings's *The Exiles of Florida,* the impassioned contemporary account of the part played by fugitive slaves in the Florida war, written by an abolitionist congressman from Ohio. Finally, I owe thanks to Albert K. Weinberg for his *Manifest Destiny,* which probes the excuses, lies, illogical arguments, and moral pieties used then—and now—to justify our nation's ruthless expansion.

The sources listed below are a selection of the books and articles I referred to in my research. In addition, I made frequent use of the files of the *Congressional Globe,* the American State Papers, *Niles' National Register,* and the Documents of the U.S. Senate and the House of Representatives, and several national and state historical journals.

ABEL, ANNIE HELOISE, *The American Indian as Slaveholder and Secessionist.* Cleveland: Clark, 1915.

ADAMS, GEORGE R., "The Caloosahatchee Massacre: Its Significance In the Second Seminole War," *Florida Historical Quarterly,* XXXXVIII (April 1970), 368–80.

BARTRAM, WILLIAM, *Travels of William Bartram,* Mark Van Doren, ed. New York: Dover, 1928.

BEALS, CARLETON, *American Earth.* Philadelphia: Lippincott, 1939.

BEMROSE, JOHN, *Reminiscences of the Second Seminole War,* John K. Mahon, ed. Gainesville: University of Florida Press, 1966.

CATLIN, GEORGE, *Letters and Notes on the Manners, Customs and Condition of the North American Indians, 1832–1839,* 2 vols. Philadelphia, 1857.

COHEN, M. M., *Notices of Florida and the Campaigns.* Gainesville: University of Florida Press, 1964.

COTTERILL, ROBERT S., *The Southern Indians: The Story of the Civilized Tribes Before Removal.* Norman: University of Oklahoma Press, 1954.

COVINGTON, JAMES W., "Cuban Bloodhounds and the Seminoles," *Florida Historical Quarterly,* XXXII (October 1954), 111–19.

———, "Migration of the Seminoles into Florida," *Florida Historical Quarterly,* XXXXVI (April 1968), 340–57.

CRANE, VERNER W., *The Southern Frontier, 1670–1732.* Ann Arbor: University of Michigan Press, 1929.

CROFFUT, W. A., ed., *Fifty Years in Camp and Field: Diary of Major General Ethan Allen Hitchcock, U.S.A.* New York, 1909.

DRIVER, HAROLD E., *Indians of North America,* 2nd ed., rev. Chicago: University of Chicago Press, 1969.

FEY, HAROLD E. AND D'ARCY MCKNICKLE, *Indians and Other Americans,* rev. ed. New York: Perennial, 1970.

FOREMAN, GRANT, *The Five Civilized Tribes.* Norman: University of Oklahoma Press, 1934.

———, *Indian Removal: The Emigration of the Five Civilized Tribes of Indians.* Norman: University of Oklahoma Press, 1953.

GARVIN, RUSSELL, "The Free Negro in Florida Before

the Civil War," *Florida Historical Quarterly,* XXXXVI (July 1967), 1–17.

GIDDINGS, JOSHUA R., *The Exiles of Florida.* Columbus, 1858.

———, *Speeches in Congress.* Boston: Jewett, 1853.

GIFFORD, JOHN C., "Five Plants Essential to the Indians and Early Settlers of Florida," *Tequesta,* No. 4 (November 1944), 36–43.

HAGAN, WILLIAM T., *American Indians.* Chicago: University of Chicago Press, 1961.

JACOBS, PAUL AND SAUL LANDAU, *To Serve the Devil,* 2 vols. New York: Vintage, 1971.

JACKSON, HELEN HUNT, *A Century of Dishonor.* New York: Harper, 1965.

JAMES, MARQUIS, *The Life of Andrew Jackson.* Indianapolis: Bobbs-Merrill, 1938.

JOSEPHY, ALVIN M., *The Patriot Chiefs.* New York: Viking Compass, 1969.

JULIAN, GEORGE W., *The Life of Joshua R. Giddings.* Chicago: McClurg, 1892.

KOWNSLAR, ALLAN O., *Manifest Destiny and Expansionism in the 1840's.* Lexington: Heath, 1967.

MCLAUGHLIN, ANDREW C., *Lewis Cass.* Boston, 1891.

MCREYNOLDS, EDWIN C., *The Seminoles.* Norman: University of Oklahoma Press, 1957.

MAHON, JOHN K., *History of the Second Seminole War.* Gainesville: University of Florida Press, 1967.

MOTTE, JACOB RHETT, *Journey into Wilderness: An Army Surgeon's Account of Life in Camp and Field During the Creek and Seminole Wars, 1836–1838,*

James F. Sunderman, ed. Gainesville: University of Florida Press, 1953.

PATRICK, REMBERT W., *Florida Fiasco: Rampant Rebels on the Georgia-Florida Border, 1810–1815.* Athens; University of Georgia Press, 1954.

PESSEN, EDWARD, *Jacksonian America: Society, Personality, and Politics.* Homewood: Dorsey, 1969.

PORTER, KENNETH W., "The Episode of Osceola's Wife: Fact or Fiction?" *Florida Historical Quarterly,* XXVI (July 1947), 92–98.

———, "Florida Slaves and Free Negroes in the Seminole War, 1835–1842," *Journal of Negro History,* XXVIII (April 1943), 390–421.

———, "John Caesar, Seminole Negro Partisan," *Journal of Negro History,* XXXI (April 1946), 190–207.

———, "The Negro Abraham," *Florida Historical Quarterly,* XXV (July 1946), 1–43.

———, "Negro Guides and Interpreters in the Early Stages of the Seminole War, December 28, 1835–March 6, 1837," *Journal of Negro History,* XXXV (April 1950), 174–82.

———, "Negroes and the Seminole War, 1817, 1818," *Journal of Negro History* XXXVI (July 1951), 249–80.

———, "Negroes and the Seminole War 1835–1842," *Journal of Southern History,* XXX (1964), 427–50.

———, "Notes Supplementary to Relations Between Negroes and Indians . . ." *Journal of Negro History,* XVIII (July 1933), 282–321.

———, "Origins of the St. Johns River Seminoles: Were

They Mikasuki?" *Florida Anthropologist,* IV (1951), 39–45.

———, "Osceola and the Negroes," *Florida Historical Quarterly,* XXX (January 1955), 235–39.

———, "Relations between Negroes and Indians Within the Present Limits of the United States," *Journal of Negro History,* XVII (July 1932), 287–367.

———, "Seminole Flight from Fort Marion," *Florida Historical Quarterly,* XXII (January 1944), 113–33.

———, "Three Fighters for Freedom: Maroons in Massachusetts; John Caesar, a Forgotten Hero of the Seminole War; Louis Pacheco," *Journal of Negro History,* XXVIII (January 1945), 53–72.

———, "Tiger Tail," *Florida Historical Quarterly,* XXIV (January 1946), 216–17.

POTTER, WOODBOURNE, *The War in Florida.* Baltimore, 1836.

PRUCHA, FRANCIS P., *American Indian Policy in the Formative Years.* Lincoln: University of Nebraska Press, 1970.

SIMMONS, WILLIAM H., *Notices of East Florida, with an Account of the Seminole Nation of Indians.* Charleston, 1822.

SMITH, W. W., *Sketches of the Second Seminole War.* Charleston, 1836.

SPRAGUE, JOHN T., *The Origin, Progress, and Conclusions of the Florida War.* Gainesville: University of Florida Press, 1964.

STAFFORD, FRANCES J., "Illegal Importations: Enforcement of the Slave Trade Laws Along the Florida Coast, 1810–1828," *Florida Historical Quarterly,* XXI (October 1967), 124–33.

TEBBEL, JOHN, *The Compact History of the Indian Wars.* New York: Hawthorn, 1966.

VAN EVERY, DALE, *Disinherited: The Lost Birthright of the American Indian.* New York: Morrow, 1966.

WASHBURN, WILCOMB E., ed., *The Indian and the White Man.* New York: New York University Press, 1964.

———, "A Moral History of Indian-White Relations," *Ethnohistory,* IV (1957), 47–61.

WEINBERG, ALBERT K., *Manifest Destiny.* Chicago: Quadrangle, 1963.

WIK, REYNOLD M., "Captain Nathaniel Wyche Hunter and the Florida Indian Campaigns, 1837–1841," *Florida Historical Quarterly,* XXXIX (July 1960), 62–75.

WILLIAMS, JOHN LEE, *The Territory of Florida.* Gainesville: University of Florida Press, 1962.

YOUNG, MARY E., "The Creek Frauds: A Study in Conscience and Corruption," *Mississippi Valley Historical Review,* XLVII (December 1955), 411–37.

———, "Indian Removal and Land Allotment: The Civilized Tribes and Jacksonian Justice," *American Historical Review,* LXIV (October 1958), 31–45.

ZINN, HOWARD, *The Politics of History.* Boston: Beacon, 1970.

Index